D1322423

OUT OF IT

OUT OF IT

how cocaine killed my brother

CLARE CAMPBELL

HODDER

British Library Cataloguing in Publication Data
A record for this book is available from the British Library

ISBN 978 0340 86362 6

Typeset in Baskerville by Avon DataSet Ltd,
Bidford on Avon, Warwickshire

Printed and bound in Great Britain by
Clays Ltd, St Ives plc

The paper and board used in this book are natural recyclable
products made from wood grown in sustainable forests.
The manufacturing processes conform to the environmental
regulations of the country of origin.

Hodder & Stoughton
A Division of Hodder Headline Ltd
338 Euston Road
London NW1 3BH
www.hodder.co.uk

'Many of us know people who take drugs, but few know serious addicts. I don't. We know friends, sensible professional people ... who sniffle cocaine in the same way they drink champagne – periodically, as one of life's little treats.'

The Times, 4 February 2005

Foreword
by Fergal Keane

I first met Bill Frost in the old reporters' room at Broadcasting House some time in the late 1980s. Bill was a languid, witty presence with a reputation as one of the more literate and clever journalists in radio news. He also had a reputation as a man who liked a drink and the company of beautiful women. In those days, before newsrooms became soulless production lines, the devil-may-care Bill was a man to be admired by the neophytes like myself. When he asked me to join him in the Hat and Stick – our favourite local watering hole – I felt privileged, as if I were being asked to enter a rather exclusive club. The details of our conversation are lost to me now. But I will never forget his charisma.

Years later, in the gardens of a hospital where Bill was being treated for alcohol and drug addiction, I reminded him of those days.

'*You* looked up to me?' he asked, clearly incredulous.

'Yes,' I replied. And I still did. But my reasons now were rather different. We had become brothers in arms. What we shared in that small hospital room was not our connection as war reporters but as struggling survivors of addiction.

I was around three years sober when I heard that Bill was in hospital. I hadn't seen him in many years though I'd heard stories about his drinking exploits. They were never nasty stories. Nor were they ever told with malice. Bill was too well liked for that. But I recognised something of my own past in the whispers about his deepening embrace of the bottle. What I didn't know then was that he had also become addicted to cocaine.

Sitting in his hospital room Bill looked haunted. He clearly registered the look of shock on my face. 'You think this is bad – you should have seen me when I came in,' he said. We spoke about the old days and then, hesitantly, our lives as alcoholics, those days of shame and regret and loneliness. There was a rueful honesty about Bill. He didn't pretend to me – as many in the early stages of recovery would – that he didn't have a problem. Bill had come through his phase of denial.

I knew nothing then of the terrible events described in this book – the entanglement in the drug world of his girlfriend's brother, the immense pressures building around Bill. I wouldn't have thought any differently of him in any case. What I saw then was a man fighting desperately hard to become well. He wanted to live and love, to be a consistent presence for the good in the lives of those who loved him. Like all of us who have felt the terrible pull of addiction, Bill was consumed by guilt. He bitterly regretted the pain his addiction had caused for others. Alcohol and drugs had taken much away from him and had caused anguish in the lives of his family, friends and lovers. That is the nature of addiction. It takes and takes until there is nothing left.

I think you need to know that lonely road before you can really understand how brave a person Bill was. In our professional lives we had both faced crazy men with guns at roadblocks in the Balkans and Africa and yet none of that could compare with what F. Scott Fitzgerald called 'the real dark night of the soul where it is always three o'clock in the morning'. Too often the alcoholic or drug addict is written off as a weak person, morally flawed. This is an understandable response to the selfishness, lies, betrayal and squalor of chronic addiction.

But I prefer the wiser and more compassionate view expressed to me by a long-time recovering alcoholic: 'We are not bad people trying to be good. We are sick people trying to be well.' I spoke with Bill by phone a few times after he left treatment. I made arrangements to meet up but he would ring and cancel at the last minute. At least he rang, I would say to myself. Then there was a phone call in which he sounded very afraid. He was at home in the flat and jittery. I was about to go to the United States on assignment and wasn't able to meet him. I told Bill to ring his counsellor and go to a 12-step meeting and repeated the mantra I lived by myself: *Stay calm. It gets better.*

Soon after that Bill was found dead. He is not the first alcoholic/addict of my acquaintance who has died from the disease of addiction. He will not be the last. The sad fact is that the majority of alcoholics and addicts don't make it through.

Bill was killed by his disease but he was one of the bravest men I knew, brave for trying again and again. Now his sister Clare has written the most moving account of the devastation caused by addiction that I can remember reading in a very long time. As I read I kept the image in my mind of Bill sitting on the edge of his bed in hospital. He was edgy and distracted that day. But most of the time he was smiling, making jokes at his own expense and, in that moment at least, hopeful that better days were coming.

Fergal Keane 2006

Prologue

My first piece of journalism, written when I was twelve, was a description of my brother, Bill. My assignment was to draw a picture in words of someone I loved or admired. Bill walked into the room at exactly the right moment, and I knew I had my subject. At that time there was no one else in the world I loved or idolised more.

I looked up eagerly, energised as always by his presence. At fifteen, he was already over six foot – lean and broad-shouldered. His dark hair, worn long over the stiff white collar of his school uniform, gave him a romantic look. His eyes were liquid hazel and full-lidded; with his dark heavy brows, it gave him a curious mix of male toughness combined with an almost feminine beauty. I thought him then, as I always did, one of the handsomest men I have ever seen.

My mother used to teasingly call him Heathcliff, but he was too intelligent and far too humorous for the comparison. No one ever made me laugh as much as Bill did. His sense of fun was puckish, and at times could be cruel, but he always regretted any hurt caused and was instantly contrite.

Thirty-five years later – when Bill was not yet fifty – I found myself on a summer's day pushing him in a wheelchair along the Fulham Road in west London. Looking down at him in sorrow and rage, I saw a man who could have been anywhere between sixty and seventy years old.

Gaunt and weighing less than 10 stone, his skin was insipid, parchment-pale, the white of his eyes a runny yolk of alcoholic poisoning. Addicted to crack cocaine, he was suffering from acute drug-induced paranoia. I looked up to see a young couple sitting in Starbucks watching us, sniggering as we struggled past, amused by the sight of what they took to be an old drunk, bickering with a relative.

After a grisly passage through the Casualty department of the Chelsea and Westminster Hospital, I left Bill to the ministrations of a concerned female psychiatrist. She told us that she could do nothing for my brother until he was sober.

We had been here before – many times over the previous two years. I knew the doctor's instinct was to be compassionate, but I needed more than that. 'Bring him back when he's clean – maybe we could assess him sometime in October,' she said wearily. Bill was now almost permanently intoxicated – either by cocaine or alcohol and frequently both. It was beyond my, or his, powers to make it otherwise. He could not feed himself. The orbit of his existence seemed to have shrunk to his flat off the North End Road market in Fulham and a garish off-licence on the corner. My brother needed help right now – and I had no idea how to find it.

Meanwhile, my four-year-old son Joseph was waiting to be collected from nursery. For a mother, and a sister, it was an impossible dilemma – to choose which of my close family needed me most at any one moment – but one that I had already been in many times before. I knew in this instance I had to go to collect my son, and looked back once more to see my brother's face – his expression flickering between the Bill I could still recognise and the crack monster who now usurped his body.

Then came a moment of hope. Later that summer, I and Bill's ex-girlfriend, the journalist Barbara Jones, managed to persuade his former employers at Times Newspapers to fund a month-long attempt at rehabilitation at the Priory, the clinic for treating addictions in south-west London. Bill had stuck it out there, and now seemed to be recovering. In late September 2000, he was discharged. Yes, he would love to come to dinner over the weekend. I made spaghetti. He never showed up.

On a chill Tuesday morning in November, almost two months later, after his phone had again gone unanswered (this time for too long), my husband, Christy, and I made an urgent trip to his flat.

I pounded on the front door. There was no response. We would have to break in. A young boy who had been passing by offered to help – clambering on to the window ledge and somehow managing to prise open the top window of the front room.

Immediately I smelt it – a pervading sickly odour of rotting vegetables and vomit. I had never been afraid of a smell before. But I was now.

'Let him be drunk, let him be drugged – just don't let him be dead. Please,' I prayed silently. Like most lapsed Catholics, I still barter with God, as Bill himself would have done when desperate.

The house was a typical Victorian villa – converted into three flats. A flight of stone steps led up to the heavy black front door, the entrance to the two upper flats. To the left, another flight of steps led steeply down to the garden flat below. The curtains of my brother's bedroom on the first floor were drawn open – but from street level it was not possible for me to see into the room.

The boy negotiated the window ledge like a gymnast, wriggled himself through the narrow opening at the top of the window, and dropped lightly down inside the room. Seconds later I heard his voice. He was banging on the inside of the deadlocked front door. I knew from the reedy pitch of his tone that he was seeing something unspeakable. But all he kept saying was, 'He's here . . . in a bad way. Open the door, OPEN THE DOOR!'

It was not until the police arrived a few minutes later that the lock on the door could finally be forced. The boy came staggering out – clearly very shocked and frightened. Then he turned to me and, suddenly no longer a boy, took me in his arms, burying my face so I could not see over his shoulder. 'I am so sorry, so sorry . . . Don't go in. Don't . . .' In that moment I knew.

Christy and a police officer entered the flat. I could not go in. My limbs felt paralysed. Whether from fear or denial, I could not see my brother's body, or be forced to confront the reality of his death. He had always been there in my life – a constant, warm, vibrant presence.

Now suddenly he was not, nor ever would be again. The enormity of my loss was overwhelming. I wanted to escape from the moment, and from myself. But there was no escape. Instead I must endure the torture of staying and waiting – staring ridiculously at the iron railings on the low wall in front of me, meticulously noting every intricate detail of their design.

Christy told me later that Bill was lying, his eyes still open as if surprised by his own sudden mortality, across a footstool. I hoped with all my heart then, and many times since, that this indicated an instantaneous death.

The boy who had found him (I never discovered his name) told me that he had found his own brother dead in similar circumstances. Whether this was some wild coincidence or simply a sign of our times, I do not know. Whichever it was, this stranger to whom I was suddenly linked by sibling death could not have been kinder or more compassionate than he was to me in those first few awful seconds of realisation.

A postmortem the following day gave the cause of Bill's death as a pulmonary embolism (a blood clot which travels from the lung to the heart) and registered his death as due to natural causes.

But the breakdown of his body and mind, from alcoholism and addiction to class A drugs, had taken several years. Nor was it a process that could in any way be categorised as 'natural'. My brother did not die from a disease of the body, but from a wasting of the soul. Like all bereaved, I feel unfairly and prematurely robbed. But that is not my reason for writing this book. Above all else, I needed to find out exactly what had happened.

PART ONE

1

It was a few days before Christmas – and less than three weeks after the death of my brother. In the time in between I had done virtually nothing – sleepwalking my way through the funeral a fortnight before – relying on Christy and our older daughters, Maria and Katy, to make the arrangements, and even the appropriate social responses.

At the dignified-enough ceremony, Bill's talents, both professional and personal, were made apparent. His journalism was lauded, his gift for friendship praised even higher. He had presented the BBC *Today* programme and *The World at One*. He had been chief reporter of *The Times* newspaper (they gave him a half-page obituary) until a turbulent departure eighteen months before.

Scores of old colleagues had left their newsrooms and offices to come to the crematorium in suburban south London on a cold Tuesday morning and to our house afterwards, each with some affectionate anecdote. Amid the comforting words there were recriminations. Perhaps we all could have done more? Why didn't you tell us? Things like this don't happen to people like Bill. But they had.

For the rest of that time I mostly sat and wept. I felt wounded, angry and absurdly resentful against everyone except my immediate family. Although losing Bill had been one of my greatest fears, I had never really believed it would actually happen. I had somehow imagined, in much the same way that he must have done, that he was in possession of superhuman powers of survival.

I kept remembering how at five years old, and much to my father's amusement, I would always follow in Bill's wake, doing whatever he told me to and hanging on his every word. Now I had a husband and three children of my own. I was surrounded and supported by those who loved me, but it didn't feel like that. Without Bill, I felt lost, back to being a small dependent child again. My brother and I had talked to one another daily, shared thoughts and feelings more freely – and sometimes more intimately – than lovers. Without Bill, I felt a piece of me was missing – abandoned, isolated and almost cosmically alone.

At night a pale-blue tarpaulin on the scaffolding outside our bedroom window flapped horribly in an apparently ceaseless rainstorm. Falling episodically into sleep, I dreamt that Bill was tapping, a lost boy, at my window to be let in. Once or twice I even got up and ran to the window, so real was the fantasy in my head. As a small child I had often been frightened at night. Bill had always come to me when I called, sitting on the bed and talking to me until the fear had gone. Now the fear was no longer imaginary, and he would never be there to comfort me again.

The idea of Christmas in the midst of such grief seemed meaningless – the happiness of others merely adding to the awfulness of Bill's absence. But I tried, for my young son Joseph's sake, to at least go through the motions of planning the celebrations. I did not want him to have to try to understand adult misery, or be made to feel guilty for enjoying himself.

It was 21 December, around eight o'clock in the evening. Christmas-tree lights glowed in the living-room. Joseph was asleep upstairs after a bath and a story.

I was in the kitchen preparing supper when I heard a sudden bang on the front door. I felt irritated. The last thing I felt like doing was facing anyone – least of all carol singers.

I carried on what I was doing, calling out to Christy to answer it. He called back, 'Leave it – they'll give up in a minute.' Instead, the bangs came louder and faster, intimidating and impossible to ignore. I felt suddenly furious. How dare they be so persistent – and at such a time?

I heard Christy swearing before opening the door – then the

sound of men's voices talking loudly and authoritatively in the hall. Now, thoroughly alarmed, I came through into the living-room to find out what was going on.

Two grave-faced men were standing there. Christy came over to stand protectively at my side. One man stepped forward, 'Clare Campbell – you are the sister of William Robert Frost?'

What now? I felt lightheaded with anxiety. 'Yes – but he's dead,' I said stupidly. 'Why? What do you want?'

Witnessing my distress, the man's features and his tone softened a little. 'Yes, we know, and I am sorry to have to intrude on you at such a time. We are officers from Her Majesty's Customs & Excise. We have reason to believe that your brother was involved in the illegal trafficking of drugs – in association with a known criminal named Kevin Hanley. We also have reason to believe that you may have in your possession documents or material, specifically a briefcase, belonging to your brother, which could assist us with our enquiries.'

It was the way policemen spoke in absurd television dramas. Things like this were not meant to happen to people like me. Yes, there was a briefcase. Bill had left it with our cousin, Sheilagh Frost, a retired GP, at her country cottage where he had stayed early last spring. He had evidently never been back to reclaim it. She had given it to me when we met at Bill's funeral two weeks before. It sat unopened by my work desk. I could not bear to pry inside.

The Customs officer continued his mechanical litany amid the Christmas tinsel: 'We would request your co-operation in handing this item over. But if you do not, I must warn you that I have in my possession a search warrant for these premises – giving us the right to confiscate whatever material we find that we think may relate to these offences . . .'

He thrust a piece of paper into my hands. At the top, in bold black ink, I read the words 'In the Central Criminal Court – Search Warrant'. Underneath, I saw Bill's name followed by my own address.

I stared at the piece of paper, my hands shaking. 'I am satisfied that there are reasonable grounds for suspecting that Kevin

Stephen Patrick Hanley and William Robert Frost have carried on or have benefited from drug-trafficking,' it read.

I sat silent. The room was swimming. I wanted it all to stop – now. The officer, this horrible intruder into my grief and pain, was talking to me again.

'I am sorry to have to do this to you at such a time, but I need to know the names of everyone currently present in this house. I must also request that you do not leave the room until my colleague and I finish our search. Is there anyone else here apart from you and your husband?'

'Only my son, Joseph – he's four.'

Momentarily embarrassed in his role as interrogator, the man's eyes flickered downwards for a second. Then the questioning began again.

'Do you have in your possession your brother's briefcase?'

'Yes, it's upstairs. I haven't looked inside it myself yet.'

'Would you please tell my colleague where he can find it?'

Instinctively, I stood up to get the case. But to my further humiliation, the Customs officer indicated, by a restraining gesture of the hand, that I must remain where I was.

I realised this action was to prevent me from removing any documents from the briefcase before bringing it downstairs, and again felt furious at the implication that I, too, was involved in some conspiracy. I felt that at any moment I would wake up and find myself safely back in the fragile-enough certainties of middle-class life. But I was wrong.

A few minutes later I found myself signing a receipt, allowing the two Customs officers to remove Bill's case – as part 'of their further investigations into the profits of drug-traffickers'.

As far as I was concerned, they were taking from me one of the pathetically few possessions I had left belonging to my only brother. I hated these two men – not just for the shock of their intrusion, but for what they seemed to be telling me of Bill's involvement in drugs. Drugs had killed him – I knew that – but what was this about trafficking and 'associating with known criminals'? The last two years of his life, the rages, the inconsolable despair, the smash-ups in every professional and personal relationship, had been bad enough. Now there was an icy logic to it. At my chiding at his drinking, Bill would always answer: 'You don't understand – I need to get out of it.' What had he done? What was he so terrified of? Suddenly I felt I must know what my interrogators knew.

The older officer gave me his card – 'Michael Torpy, HM Customs & Excise, National Investigation Service'. His colleague, David Terrell, managed a thin smile as his eager eyes took in the room and its contents – pictures of our children, the computer on which I did my work. Would they be taking that away too? They began to ask more questions. The tone was blander, more conversational.

'What did I know of Bill Frost's relationship with Hanley?'

I mumbled something: 'Alex Hanley is Kevin Hanley's older sister. Alex was Bill's girlfriend, had been for about five years. They'd all gone away a few times, for family holidays. There's a mother, Bridget, who lives in Fulham. I had met them . . . I had no idea. What is this all about?'

Out it all came, slowly at first. Torpy told us what it was they were looking for – evidence that my brother had been laundering money for Kevin Hanley, either by buying properties under a false name, or opening offshore accounts to hide illegal profits.

Perhaps I should also know, he continued, that Customs had been operating a surveillance operation on the movements of both Kevin and his wife, Lena, over a period of the previous two years. Had they watched Alex – Bill's girlfriend? Had they watched me – his sister? Torpy did not know – or would not say. I was gasping for breath. I felt like screaming: 'Bill, tell me what you've done!' He would not then. He could not do so now.

Then Torpy told me, almost casually, that Customs officers had been due to call on Bill at his flat to interview him – the day after we had broken in and found his body.

Horrible conspiracies flashed through my head. Could Bill have known, and have taken his own life as a means of escape? Or was it possible that someone else had known, someone who could not afford for my brother to be questioned in such a vulnerable mental state?

I tried to think back to the arrival of the policeman at Bill's flat. Christy had said the officer checked for signs of a break-in, or of any evidence that Bill had not been alone at the time of his death.

Had someone either murdered Bill, or given him sufficient drugs or alcohol to do the job for them? Bill had told me in a phone call just two days before his death (it was the last time we spoke together) that he had not been drinking – and I had just about believed him. Yet the police had found vodka bottles in the flat – there was always lots of vodka in the flat.

I realised now that I might never find out the answers. A postmortem had been carried out the day after we had found my brother dead. It said his death was due to natural causes. No one had mentioned a toxicology report, and as far as I knew no such investigation had been made.

A terrible anger suffused me – body and soul. I wanted desperately to be left alone to think, to work this out for myself. Why couldn't these men realise that and just *go*?

Officer Torpy was clearly as uncomfortable about his presence in my home as I was. He apologised again for his intrusion before he and his colleague finally lumbered out of the house mumbling condolences, assuring me as they did so that they would return my brother's briefcase as soon as they had finished with it. They had what they wanted. We seemed innocent enough for now.

As the front door slammed behind them, I thought: 'My brother is dead and now my house has just been raided for evidence that he was a drug-trafficker.' I put my hands up to cover my face, trying to shut everything out. Christy came back into the room and put his arms around me. I was beyond tears by now, numbed into submission by shock.

All I wanted was for my brother to be alive again, even as a drunk or a junkie, just so long as he was physically there beside me. I remembered the way he used to hold my hand when we talked, a childhood habit of affection that he never outgrew.

The events that had engulfed my family made me question all that I had ever taken for granted about the security and happiness of those closest to me. I myself had changed completely – both by my loss, and my own forced entry into what Bill himself often referred to as 'mirror-world': a moral landscape where the values we had both been brought up to respect were totally reversed.

I had gone through a rite of passage. I was now in possession of knowledge that I most surely did not want to know but that, one day, would have to be acted upon.

The decision to embark on a journey that would draw me further into this netherworld was not an easy one, and it took me several years to summon up the courage. Although I had been assured of the help both of Bill's friends and colleagues in journalism – and by the investigating officers in the case – I had also been warned that I might be bringing my safety and that of my family under threat.

But I had no option. Loving Bill as I did, I had to find out why he fell so far. I had to know why he died. Like it or not, my brother's destiny stalked my own.

2

Those who have analysed the cycle of grief are right: denial, followed by anger and, maybe at the end, acceptance. The weeks and months after my brother's death ran to the textbook 'grief script', fastforwarded only a little by the Customs raid. I more or less sleepwalked through the funeral – and I was still anaesthetised when the investigators came trampling into my house. I was then very angry – furious with Bill, full of rage at those who I thought had somehow colluded in his death. Most of all, I was angry with myself. But in those first six months after his death, it was all about denial.

How could it be possible that Bill was dead? What was this nonsense about my brother and drug-trafficking? If I wanted to know more, and at that point I didn't, where could I look? Who could I ask? There was nothing about Kevin Hanley in the papers. After the funeral, Alex and her family seemed to have disappeared like wraiths. Every morning I would wake up convinced it was all a malign dream.

There was a memorial service to plan; Bill's own employers, Times Newspapers, thought it very appropriate. There were soothing meetings with sympathetic executives and kindly clergymen. There was music to choose, readings from Bill's journalism to prepare. Colleagues would love to help, to honour their lost friend. It was as if Bill had been cut down by crossfire in a war zone. They were comforting and crass all at once. 'What happened to Bill?' they asked. 'We all seem to have rather lost touch.' One even asked me to write a life-story of his last two years, to send as a kind of round-robin. I could not do so – for one simple reason. I myself did not know 'what had happened to Bill'. Much later, I woke up one morning determined to find out.

I was embarking on a double journey. The first was into my own past, or at least that part I had shared with the brother I knew and loved. The second was down a dark road I did not know.

Bill, when he was alive, would never tell me the point along that road at which he lost his moral compass. In those numb weeks after his death, all the evidence that seemed to be left of why and how he died was a jumble of papers, the ones in the briefcase that I could not bear to look inside. Now the Customs investigators had spirited even that away.

The briefcase itself was strange. It was made of transparent plastic and branded with the logo of 'Paul and Shark', the retailers of yachting clothes and accessories. It seemed cold and menacing; its tacky glamour alien to Bill's own innate sense of taste. And my brother, as far as I knew, had never been interested in yachts. How did the Customs officers know the briefcase was at my house? Our cousin Sheilagh had informed them, so she would tell me later. Investigators had been to visit her in deepest Sussex the day before. But how did Customs know it was there in the first place, that it existed at all? Had they been watching her house? No one would ever give me a straight answer to that one. Eventually I would find out.

A few months later, Customs returned the briefcase. At last I could look inside – bank and credit card statements, airline ticket stubs, final demands, a curious leasing agreement on a holiday caravan. The papers told me nothing that I could understand.

But Bill had left something else. While in the Priory he had compiled a kind of life-story – a standard therapeutic technique in addiction treatment. It was written in ballpoint on tatty lined paper like a schoolboy essay. Christy had retrieved it from the flat and given it to me, unread, he assured me, by him. I could not yet summon the courage to read it. One day I would.

I have no misgivings about using some of it in this narrative. Many authors have written accounts of their descent into addiction – after they recovered. Bill didn't make it. His words, written when sober, are insightful and full of contrition for what he did to those he loved. I found his accounts both heart-rending and at the same time strangely comforting. It was the last story he ever wrote in a career of writing stories. Let him, I thought, have his say.

By the time I found the strength to read Bill's confessional 'biography', he had been dead for over a year. Sitting at my desk one afternoon, I picked it up and began to read.

I opened the blue and white Priory Hospital folder. On the cover was printed 'Galsworthy Lodge – Step One', and my brother's name and the date of admission were scribbled in biro across the top.

Inside was a brief printed explanation that these 'steps' were designed to help him 'accept his problem and rebuild his life'. I wondered whether I really wanted to continue reading – knowing that Bill was unable to do either, wasn't I just inviting further miserable reflections on why? But perhaps I might learn something about what was going on inside Bill's head. It was worth a try. Tucked inside the folder was the handwritten 'biography'.

It began at the beginning: 'I was born to middle-class Irish parents in 1950. The family home in Clapham stood in the midst of a post-war moonscape – there were Blitz reminders everywhere. I remember a happy childhood; rambling through the rubble in search of treasures and playing on the anti-aircraft battery positions on Clapham Common . . .'

As I read on, my first thought was that I didn't recognise this person. All the facts were there – our family background, the happy childhood seaside holidays, school, teenage rebellion, the intimacy of his relationship with me. But somehow it was not the Bill I knew. It was written as if he were trying to convince an audience rather than in his real voice. There were episodes I knew were fantasy or a convenient rearranging of the facts. Was Bill even now still holding something of himself back?

The biography and the accompanying therapy notes told me a great deal about his descent into addiction and his struggle to get better – but very little about how and why he lost the fight. They said nothing at all about 'drug-trafficking'.

The Customs investigators meanwhile seemed to have lost interest in me. The plaudits of his colleagues had gone quiet. Alex had seemingly vanished (there had been one phone call on the first anniversary of his death). Meanwhile, I was left with the mournful task of recovering bits of his furniture from a lock-up container in the Cotswolds into which they had vanished in one of the shambolic reshuffles of his living arrangements. I opened the horrible metal doors to find intimate chunks of our childhood packed inside. My mother's desk. Some family photographs.

There was at that time still a presiding mystery. What had happened to Kevin Hanley? He seemed to have disappeared into thin air. It transpired there was a reason. My own small eve-of-Christmas 2000 drama, I would discover much later, was a tiny part of a Customs and police operation that had already been in play for over three years. When the Customs' 'knock' came on my door, the global investigation had another eighteen months to run. Its sensitivity and legal complexity meant it was all kept secret. Gagging orders were placed on any newspaper that got a sniff of the story. It was called 'Operation Extend'.

Bill had told me so little when he was alive. I knew that Kevin had been picked up by the Metropolitan Police in November 1998 – my brother had at least told me that. I remembered the night it happened – when Bill had stumbled through our doorway out of his head on drugs and booze, but clearly terrified of something or someone. 'What is it?' I had pleaded with him, 'Why are you doing this?'

'You don't want to know,' he replied. 'You don't want to go there.'

Bill had refused to talk about it any further, just as he had earlier refused to explain the bizarre and menacing people I had encountered on my increasingly reluctant visits to his house a few streets away from my own in Wandsworth, south London.

'What's happened to Kevin?' I would ask my brother innocently enough in our anguish-filled meetings in the months that followed. 'Is it something to do with him – is that what this is all about?'

Bill would grimace and grip my hand – his eyes almost

subterranean in their too large sockets – then suddenly bark: 'You don't understand what I have done for him. You don't know what I've done for that family . . .' But when I pressed him to tell me more, he would look doubtful, muttering: 'Better not . . .', reaching for another retch-inducing red-top Marlboro and letting go of my hand.

I also knew vaguely at the time – it was now early 1999 – that Kevin's wife Lena had also been taken into custody a month or so after Kevin's arrest. I found out later that Bill had been asked to go to court and give some kind of character reference. I also knew Bill had gone several times to see Kevin while he was held on remand, but just where this was I was not sure. Bill had got incoherently drunk on each occasion. All Bill would indicate to me in periods of sobriety was that the charges against Hanley were something to do with drug-dealing, and that he had strongly advised him to plead guilty.

Other than Kevin and Lena, no other defendants or anyone else involved were ever mentioned by Bill. He was already shutting down. Plans for next week, even the next day, were meaningless. Bill was abdicating from the real world. He stopped reading newspapers. He seemed scared of the telephone. If it rang when I was with him in the flat on some mission to try and clean him up, he would simply pull it out of the wall. His calls to me, desperate, pleading, accusing, all at once, had begun to come from strange numbers – public phone boxes. 'For fuck's sake, Clare, not on an open line,' he would growl whenever I dared to ask about Kevin.

'Don't talk about that,' he would say when I accusingly mentioned his own evident use of drugs. The line would go dead as he hung up, followed by another call from him a few minutes later – with the same impossible mix of crying for help and conspiratorial urging to say nothing and do nothing.

Something huge and menacing was happening, but there was nothing to indicate what it was. Bill would not, or could not, tell me. The newspapers hardly reported a glimmer – not when Bill was alive, nor for nearly two years after his death.

There were, I would discover much later, brief press mentions at the time, February 1999, of a 'cocaine bust' at a lock-up garage in Essex and committal proceedings after a wave of arrests. Those charged bore a curious assortment of South American and English/Irish-sounding names. 'Hanley' had not been among them. I never spotted the reports; they would have been meaningless to me anyway. And if any of Bill's newspaper colleagues were aware of them, they were not telling.

When Kevin's own trial had begun with a preliminary hearing at the Old Bailey on 24 March 2000, the reporting restrictions imposed by the judge were absolute. I would find out why it was so secret later. Kevin changed his plea to guilty on the very eve of going into the dock on charges of 'importation and conspiracy to supply'.

The trial of the other conspirators had begun in May 2000 in a closed special court next to Belmarsh high-security prison, ringed by armed police. There were more trials in Bristol and Southampton. All were *in camera*, nothing was made public, even the fact that they were taking place was secret.

At that time, if Bill had wanted to tell me anything, to confess, to confide, to ask for my or anyone else's help or forgiveness, by then he was barely able to pick up a telephone.

No verdict on any individual was made public until the last of sixteen defendants had been tried and sentenced. The facts about 'Operation Extend', and the trials to which it led, would not emerge until the last of five separate legal proceedings had concluded in June 2002. By then, Bill had been dead for almost two years.

The Customs raid on my house should have prepared me for more shocks, but I was not ready for this. According to the investigating officers, Kevin Hanley and others had been part of the 'most prolific and successful drug-smuggling organisation ever to target the United Kingdom'. It stretched from Colombia, via the Caribbean, right across the world. Ocean-going yachts had been used to ferry cocaine across the Atlantic – tons of it – to be transferred at sea on to innocent-looking pleasure craft which would offload the cargo at leisure in the affluent marinas and harbours of the south coast of England.

A Customs investigator would later describe Kevin Hanley to me as 'the most significant wholesaler of cocaine in London'. Bill, at this time, was referring to Kevin as 'the brother-in-law'.

It was not just about drugs – British horse racing had also been corrupted by this criminal organisation's alleged demon-king: 'Brian Brendon Wright'. He was a beefy, middle-aged, Irish-born Londoner, with a string of celebrity friends and a habit of entertaining jockeys to 'golf weekends' in Spain and to his table at the nightclub Tramp.

The press were going to get very excited about that. But as far as HM Customs & Excise were concerned, the alleged race-fixing was a front for laundering money made in drugs. Bags of money. Offshore accounts, property bought in phoney names – the kind of stuff the Customs officers told me they were looking for when they raided my house looking for Bill's briefcase.

What had my brother really done? Whatever had led him into the mirror-world?

3

Who could I ask? Who would tell me what really happened to my brother? I would talk to Bill's friends and colleagues, I would go to his ex-wife Ruth, to his last girlfriend, Alex Hanley, visit Kevin in prison, even track down Brian Brendon Wright if that was necessary – whatever, or whoever, it took.

All I had was HM Customs' self-congratulatory statement released at the end of the trials in the summer of 2002. As far as my own quest for the facts was concerned, it posed as many questions as it gave answers. Bill was never mentioned. The media coverage had added very little in the way of hard information.

'The men who excited most interest were Brian Wright junior and a man investigators identified as Kevin Hanley,' reported the *Evening Standard*. The article continued: 'Wright junior was his father's right-hand man, and Hanley, 39, organised deliveries and sold the cocaine to dealers in Britain. In November 1998 Hanley was arrested driving through London with 29 kg of cocaine in the boot of his car. The drugs were part of a major consignment and Wright immediately ordered the suspension of all operations . . .'

I meanwhile found earlier reports in Irish and local English newspapers, plus snippets from the internet. There was not much there either – just some stuff about a converted trawler, the *Sea Mist*, being impounded in Cork harbour in 1996 and being found stuffed with cocaine.

The forces of the law had come prying into my life, and I would start by prying into what they really knew. I applied to the court for a transcript of Kevin Hanley's trial, but was informed by officials that its release remained at the discretion of the judge.

Anyway, so I was told, Hanley had simply pleaded guilty and was later sentenced. No evidence was presented and there was no cross-examination. The transcript would not tell me much.

But there was another reason for the continuing secrecy. Brian Brendon Wright and other suspects were still at large, and huge quantities of 'dirty money' were allegedly hidden somewhere. The sensitivity about what had been said in the trials remained intense, lest its publication prejudice proceedings against those still to be brought to justice and, so I supposed, the hunt for their criminal proceeds.

The judge would not be moved. I could not see the transcript. 'It's very unusual,' a court official told me, 'this reluctance to provide information on a trial.' It was indicated that I might in some way be being viewed as an accomplice – seeking some legal loophole as grounds for an appeal – or acting as a front to get my hands on the money. For now at least, it seemed a dead-end.

I decided on another route in my search. On a hot afternoon in September 2004, nearly four years after my brother's death, I picked up the phone and rang our Christmas inquisitor, Customs investigator Mike Torpy. He was now working for London Regional Asset Recovery, a Home Office unit concerned with tracing the proceeds of crime. That was his side of the operation – tracking down dirty money after criminal convictions. Another and much more secretive side of HM Customs, I would discover, had been involved in bringing the conspirators to justice in the first place. Getting those officers to talk to me would prove far more difficult.

I had spoken to Mike Torpy several times over the intervening months and had found him sympathetic. I told him I was writing a book about what had happened to Bill, and I could tell that he wanted to help me – as I guessed he had done since that December night three years earlier. Torpy began to speak, slowly at first, carefully choosing his words as he recalled the events of five years earlier:

'It was a huge case of course, Operation Extend, and we are rightly proud of it. Took years of investigation and manhours to trap them . . . Second longest trial in British legal history and convicted fifteen people here and in the US . . . and a lot of good came out of it, too. We smashed a big drugs ring.

'Of course, you never get near the Colombian end,' he said. 'That's impossible. Cut off one tentacle and another grows. But at least we did something.

'Wright's still at large of course, but he has a heart condition and isn't likely to last long.

'We know your brother was being used by them,' he said, 'leasing property for Hanley in his name . . . probably being given drugs in return . . . and of course once he had done that, there was really no way out for Bill. He wouldn't have been able to tell anyone without getting into trouble himself.

'I just wish I had had the chance to interview your brother before he died,' Torpy continued. 'Not that they would have trusted him with laundering any substantial amounts. He was pretty much out of control by then, wasn't he?'

Torpy sensed my stab of grief. 'Sorry. Of course I didn't mean to . . .'

'Yes, yes. I suppose he was.'

'We never got Kevin's money anyway,' he continued. 'The search for that has gone dead for the time being – probably stashed away in some Swiss bank account.'

If it was, I certainly didn't know.

My conversations with Mike Torpy always had an edge. He would tell me something, and I often – before I realised – would let something slip in return. I think we both knew we were bartering information. For example, he was keen at one stage to know whether Bill had ever 'visited the New Forest'. I said that I thought he had on several occasions.

I knew also that Bill was somehow involved with a 'caravan' at a leisure park on the Sussex coast at Pagham, near Chichester. It was some sort of holiday home for Alex's mother, Bridget, so Bill had told me at the time. Torpy seemed to know all about it.

'Did you ever go to the caravan site?' he said. 'Luxurious place it was, heated swimming pools, health club, sauna, the lot. Not your usual tacky place at all . . .'

No, I thought, I had never been there – but well remembered the ranting calls I had received from Bill at the time:

'I don't know why I am here in this bloody, fucking place. I tell you, Clare, I can't stand much more of this, I really can't . . . They are driving me mad, the lot of them,' he had said. 'Especially Lena . . . and Alex. Bridget is here too, looking after Max . . .'

Mike Torpy had a slightly different picture of cosy domesticity at Church Farm holiday village: 'The men used to send the women down there when they were off on a big smuggling operation,' he told me. 'They would take the children with them and stay there until the men told them to come back.'

I wondered again how Mike Torpy himself had always seemed so willing to trust me. Kevin Hanley clearly liked to keep business in the family and I was Bill's sister. In more normal times, Bill and I had spoken daily on the phone as well as frequently visiting one another. Bill and Alex had lived just round the corner from us, and after my son Joseph was born, Bill had often called in on his way back from work. How did Customs know that I had never been involved? Had anyone checked up on me?

'No, you and your family were never under surveillance,' Torpy said. 'You were not your brother's keeper after all. But we needed hard evidence, and when we came to you that night in December after Bill's death and asked for the briefcase, you might have said "No". Had you done so, there would have been nothing we could do. We could not afford to take that chance. So we had to have a search warrant for your property just to make certain.'

I asked Torpy whether the investigating officers involved on the original case would be permitted to speak to me. He sighed: 'Well, it's all a bit difficult. What I am not sure of is how much information you would be given access to that is not already in the public domain,' he said wearily. He suggested I contact the Customs Press Office and copy the letter to Paul Evans, the Head of Investigations. 'He's a former MI6 man and will understand. After all, at the end of the day it is all good publicity for HM C & E.'

'Is it?' I thought as I put down the phone. If only I had been able to see it like that.

Less than twenty-four hours later, I got a call from a female Press Officer who sounded simultaneously conciliatory, urgent and guarded:

'About your letter, Ms Campbell. Paul Evans received his copy this morning, before I got mine actually. He contacted me straightaway . . . he is naturally very concerned . . . we all are . . . but whether or not you will be able to talk to any of the officers, though, is another matter . . .

'May I just ask you a few further questions about your brother and what happened?' she continued. 'I apologise if you find any of this distressing . . .'

'No, it's fine,' I replied, sounding as matter-of-fact as I could.

She continued: 'First of all, you mention your brother dying as a result of his involvement in this case. What was the cause of death? Was there a coroner's report? Was anyone else on the premises? Were the police involved? Which station?'

I suddenly felt I had got it wrong. All I had done with my prying and poking was to reawaken the horrors of Bill's death. Were Customs really going to tell me anything I did not know already?

The fourth anniversary of Bill's death passed; his press card photo, which I always kept on my desk, stared back at me each day as I sat down to start work. I was struck by how relaxed and handsome he looked. I glanced at the date on the card – March 1998. That was only two years before Bill died. What had happened that could have caused such a catastrophic decline? Worse still, it was starting to look as if I might never find out.

In January 2005 I was invited to attend a meeting at HM Treasury in Whitehall. I waited in the lobby by a huge Edwardian fireplace. It was all very grand, all very serious. I was ushered through security booths to a palatial meeting room overlooking the House of Commons. Across the oak table were Jan Marszewski, Press Officer, Law Enforcement HM Customs & Excise, and Anil Gogna, the Chief Investigating Officer on Operation Extend. They spoke stiffly at first – stuff about 'Public Interest Immunity', and not saying anything that might reveal their methods of operation. It seemed to involve a lot of chasing people around in taxis.

Then the conversation warmed up. They relaxed, became friendlier – flattered perhaps that a journalist should take an interest in their work. Out it all came – a calm, professional narrative of the life and crimes of Kevin Stephen Patrick Hanley and his involvement, or otherwise, with William Robert Frost. I listened for two hours, scribbling in a notebook. Some of it I knew already, but some of what I heard was jaw-dropping. One episode was heartbreaking.

'Look, look,' I said as I compared what they were telling me with what I knew of Bill's decline, 'that date fits, so does that.'

A sudden sense of panic gripped me. The aching loss I felt, even after four years, was always there – but now the volume was turned right up, and a voice inside me was screaming: 'Why didn't you do more to save him?'

I didn't know, I didn't know . . . but I did now.

I felt as if someone had ripped a blindfold from my eyes – one that had been there since Bill had first become involved with Alex Hanley's brother almost ten years earlier. Everything about Bill's story looked different now. It had not been simply 'drink and drugs' that had killed my brother. He had been terrified of being incriminated in the very drug-trafficking conspiracy that was feeding half of London's addiction and, I had then to suppose, his own.

I composed myself, ordered my notes, and thanked them for their frankness. Was there anything more I might see on the background to Operation Extend?

'There is something,' said Anil, 'I think we might be able to let you have it.' Two days later, a 100-page document arrived in my e-mail inbox.

Now I could see it. The bust-ups and disasters that marked Bill's fall, each ratchet downwards, matched a step in the parallel unfolding drama of crime, detection and retribution. I was beginning to get it now.

4

But there was another and deeper thought troubling me. Perhaps my brother's destiny was already out there waiting – death merely loitering at the fatal turn in the road. Perhaps he really had, as he would tell me without boasting, seen too many horrible things as a front-line war correspondent to find any comfort in 'normal' life.

After Bill's death, colleagues who had been alongside him in the Lebanon, Northern Ireland, Bosnia, and other harrowing assignments, recalled that while others would go on for hours about the horrors they had witnessed as if it were some kind of gruesome competition, Bill avoided what he regarded as a form of personal self-aggrandizement at all costs.

Just once, and only because I asked him directly while we were talking one night in a wine bar together, did he describe an incident that had occurred while he was reporting for *The Times* in Bosnia in 1992.

'We drove into what at first seemed a deserted village,' he told me. 'I happened to glance up and saw a pale shape spread-eagled against the pitched roof of a house.

'As we got nearer I recognised what it was – a man's body crucified on the charred remains of his home. Then we all started looking around us. There were men's corpses everywhere, all massacred in exactly the same manner.

'We were about to leave when I heard the sound of a woman's voice, weeping. Entering one of the houses, I found an elderly blind woman bent low over the body I could only think must be that of her son. He had terrible open wounds down either side and had clearly been dead for some hours.

'I went to put my arm around her to comfort her. She reached out to me in return, talking and crying all the time. Then before I could stop her she snatched hold of my hands and plunged them into her son's body. I was appalled, but so shocked I was paralysed for several minutes. I didn't know what to do to help her and just stood there, helpless, realising there was nothing I could do.'

Throughout his narrative, Bill managed to maintain the calm, clear tones of the experienced war correspondent, as if doing a piece for radio. Only when he had reached the end of his story did his voice falter. For a few seconds the line of his mouth contorted as if he were struggling with some internal pain. He winced, and then, a crucial indicator of what was already beginning to happen to him, he reached forward and drank a whole glass of wine in one swallow.

Alcohol as an anaesthetic – he was using it to blot out the horrors of other people's suffering. Soon he would be using it to blot out his own. The pain of the moment might have seemed to Bill to have passed with that first heavy gulp of wine, later perhaps in a snort of cocaine, but all it had really done was sink down into a deeper, darker corner of his mind.

He had survived the physical dangers of war-reporting more or less intact. I could not even begin to comprehend what damage it might have done inside. Where, when and how had Bill fatally mislaid that all-important instinct for self-preservation? To find out, I had to go on searching deep into my brother's past.

His instinct for self-preservation was certainly still there when, after leaving Dulwich College in 1968 with, as a result of too much partying and too little study, lower A-level grades than had been predicted, Bill 'pulled himself up by his bootstraps', as our Uncle Harry bluntly put it, to gain himself a scholarship to read English at Pembroke College, Oxford.

Inseparable as we had always been, I insisted on accompanying Bill on the journey to his relocation, along with his precious stereo system and his two prized Tommy Nutter suits (one orange velvet and the other a pinstriped silk), to his new lodgings – a damp, grey, stone college room at the top of a dark wooden staircase.

Oxford was not a happy experience for Bill who detested the all-male atmosphere of the college – although he made some very close and lasting friendships, including those with my future husband, Christy Campbell, and with the writer and *Daily Telegraph* foreign correspondent, Patrick Bishop.

'Bill was this glamorous figure living three doors down from me – dashing, witty and good-looking,' Patrick recalled. 'He and his friend, Christy, were always a double act, an amazing duo arriving in the local pub together like Withnail and I.'

I missed my brother viscerally during those first few months and frequently visited him in Oxford, often accompanied by his long-term girlfriend, Margaret Cowell, an art student, who was then studying at Ravensbourne College in Kent.

Bill had first met Margaret at the age of fifteen, so they had by this stage been together for nearly five years. I liked Margaret, as well as admiring her in the way that younger girls often look up to those who, although only a few years older than themselves, seem already so much more in command of the intricate skills of managing men, fashion and make-up.

She was also very humorous, and she and Bill devised their own private language from the small ads in *Dalton's Weekly* – those strange shorthand urgings on the Underground to 'Gt a Gd Jb with Mo Pa' (get a good job with more pay) – effectively preventing either set of parents from understanding their intimate conversations. From the beginning of their relationship, Bill regularly smoked cannabis – as did all our friends. It was, as I remember, mainly supplied by a friend of Bill's from Dulwich College, who later, while still only in his early twenties, was to serve time in prison for dealing.

I myself started smoking the drug in my mid-teens and from then on spent a lot of time in the company of Bill and his friends. Bill certainly did not seem to show any addictive tendencies and – in a curious reversal of what was to follow – frequently acted as a restraining influence where drugs and his younger sister were concerned.

In spite of my closeness to Bill, I was not in the least bit jealous of Margaret, and completely accepted both her role in his life and in my own. But Bill did not take such a tolerant view of any potential transfer of my allegiance to another male.

Any serious boyfriend of mine had, like the rutting of young stags, to first see off the dominant male. In Bill's case this was to prove so hard that it was not until I married his friend, Christy, that I witnessed any sign that my brother might be willing to let me go and become another man's wife.

Bill and Margaret split up during his second year at university when Bill went off on a long holiday to California by himself. Somehow, in spite of having left Margaret behind, he had expected her to remain the loyal girlfriend waiting at home.

What happened was not surprising. Margaret had an affair with an old school friend of Bill's, who at the time was a student at Warwick University. Losing his girlfriend to a rival was obviously a blow to Bill's ego, but it also perhaps did a lot more than that – it planted the seeds of the obsessional jealousy that was later in his life, once his mind had become damaged by drugs, to torment him horribly.

I made another discovery that explained something else in my search along the trail to Bill's addiction. He himself had an affair while in America – with a much older woman, who introduced him to cocaine. The episode was spelled out almost thirty years later in his confessional biography written at the Priory. She was, he wrote: 'An American, twice my age, I met at a party after my break-up with Margaret. By comparison with my previous girlfriends, she seemed so sophisticated . . .

'One night at her flat I remember with great clarity. Before we went to bed she produced a small rectangular packet, opened it carefully, and began scraping the white powder it contained into neat lines on the glass on the table.

'She sniffed two before offering me a cut-down straw. Curious and not wishing to appear gauche, I followed her example. Seconds later the rush hit. I had found a new sensation and I loved it – better than grass, hash, speed, Mandrax or acid. And the sex, well, it just seemed to go on for ever.'

An experience soon afterwards was clearly not so blissful: 'On 14 February 1972 my benevolent view of drugs was to be dramatically recast,' he wrote. 'I took some very strong acid which wrecked me. I was twitching, sweating and panicking. When the effects eventually wore off I vowed never to mess with acid again. I had seen the dark side, the skull beneath the skin – and it had scared the daylights out of me.

'A few days later I smoked a spliff before going to bed – good, mellow Afghan or so I thought. I climbed under the sheets and read for a while before turning out the light.

'I soon drifted off but woke in a sweaty panic minutes later with the sensation that I was falling through space. I jumped up out of bed and paced the room, breathing in shallow gasps. It was what I later came to know as a panic attack – and I guessed was the afterburn of the acid.

'For months after this I remained pathologically scared of drugs, and sneered at alcohol, throwing myself into my studies as a diversion.'

And he did. His academic results were excellent, gaining an 2:1 in English Literature at the end of his three years at Oxford. Talented, handsome and self-confident, his minor dalliance with drugs seemed insignificant, a rite of passage on the route to adulthood. No one doubted for a second that Bill would succeed in whatever he chose to do.

5

If I had expected Bill's time at university to have separated us, it was not to be so. We remained exceptionally close – sometimes to the detriment of my relationships with boyfriends, who resented the complexity of such sibling intimacy. Although always successful with women, Bill himself did not seem to meet anyone who came near to replacing Margaret in his life.

After graduating in 1973, Bill started a job as a trainee reporter on *Commercial Motor*, the transport trade magazine; it was hardly glamorous, but gave him a tough and rumbustious grounding in the practicalities of journalism. Bill was a born communicator, and had a fascination and a skill with words that was as integral a part of him as the colour of eyes. Both in conversation, and on paper, he never lost the ability to shock, amuse and amaze his audience.

While at *Commercial Motor* Bill learnt both shorthand and court reporting – both skills that were useful to him when applying, two years later in 1975, to join the ferociously competitive BBC graduate trainee scheme.

Needless to say, he got in. My brother had a talent for getting what he wanted. Bill had found his métier in a career that would see him soar, harnessing that restless energy that, unless channelled creatively, so often hovered around him like a malevolent poltergeist.

Soon after this period I started my relationship with his old Oxford friend, Christy Campbell, then working in a Soho magazine publishing company. A marriage proposal followed and I accepted. Bill was pleased if somewhat reticent. But my actions, it seemed, could also set the pattern for his. If I was going to marry and settle down, why shouldn't he?

Within three months of my wedding, Bill had started going out with Ruth Cowell, the elder sister of his former girlfriend, Margaret. He had known her for years, of course, and confided in me that he had always been slightly in awe of her cool poise and quiet self-confidence.

Ruth was small-boned, dark and glamorous with olive skin and an almost asiatic beauty. She was also sensitive, intuitive and a talented artist in her own right, then working as an art historian at the Wallace Collection in London.

Very early on in their relationship Bill was declaring his intention to marry her as soon as possible. Like everything about my brother, his love could seem excessive, and Ruth was at first both rather overwhelmed and slightly wary. But his talent for getting what he wanted did not fail him this time either. The wedding took place not far from her family home in Hayes, at Tunbridge Wells Registry Office, on 18 March 1977.

The first six months of their married life could not have contrasted more starkly with my own. While I became pregnant with twins, struggling between work and smashing down walls of our modest Victorian terrace house, Bill and Ruth simply got out their Habitat starter pack, unwrapped their colour co-ordinated linen and planned their next holiday. Setting up home, a rented cottage near Toad Rock in Tunbridge Wells, they spent lavishly – on meals out, self-adornment and weekends away. I envied them desperately. But perhaps, looking back, the envy was mutual.

By now I was nearly seven months pregnant. Bill was very excited about the prospect of becoming an uncle, and when my twin daughters, Maria and Katy, were born three months later he came straight from the BBC that evening to visit me in hospital, delightedly dubbing his nieces 'Midwich Cuckoos' as he received their first, fierce turquoise stare.

Bill's career at the BBC was beginning to really take off. He was appointed as a lobby correspondent at the House of Commons, and on 30 March 1979 he witnessed and reported first-hand on the murder of the Tory MP Airey Neave, then Shadow Secretary for Northern Ireland. Bill was on the way to the car park to go home when the INLA bomb went off. He ran towards the sound of the explosion – to discover the desperately injured Neave trapped still alive inside his car.

As an ambulance sped the victim to hospital where he later died from his injuries, Bill, still in the House of Commons car park, gave a shaken and white-faced account of what he had seen straight to camera.

At home with my parents that evening, we switched on the television for the news without knowing anything of Bill's involvement in the drama. Bill's on-screen delivery was superb, his shock and fear at the tragedy he had just witnessed adding to the immediacy and effectiveness of his reporting.

These things did not go unrecognised or unrewarded at the BBC and within a short time Bill was presenting, as well as reporting for, the *Today* programme on Radio 4, *PM*, and the *World at One*. Here he met and quickly became friends with such radio names as John Timpson, Brian Redhead, Gordon Clough and James Naughtie. Veteran Parliamentary Correspondent John Cole, who Bill worked with at the House of Commons, took my brother under his owlish avuncular wing immediately, as did Denis Murray, who also became a good friend to Bill during their stints reporting together on Northern Ireland.

Bill described in his confessional diary his life with some of Belfast's press corps: 'consisting of countless nights in pubs and clubs after covering yet another bombing, sniper attack or cruel sectarian murder'. Yet, he claimed, 'their boozing paled to insignificance when compared with their counterparts in Beirut'.

Lebanon at the height of the civil war was Bill's next major foreign assignment. It was a country he came to feel an affinity with even though just being there, by his own admission, 'scared him witless'. But he was already finding a way around the fear for he spoke in his confessional diary for the first time of: 'buying 90% pure cocaine from the bent pharmacist around the corner from the Commodore – the West Beirut hotel favoured by the international press corps'.

Meeting up on his return, he would tell me of his loneliness while away, but also how he identified with a famous line from the film *Apocalypse Now*, which he said summed up not just his own but every war reporter's ambiguous attitude: 'When I'm there I want to be home and when I'm home I want to be there.'

If he was taking drugs at this time, I did not know much about it. If he drank too much, so did everyone else. He was thirty years old. His life was glamorous, exciting; I was hugely envious. Bill and Ruth took regular three-week sybaritic sojourns in the Caribbean. I pushed a double baby buggy to the swing-park.

I never saw Bill and Ruth together looking anything but smiling and affectionate, Ruth's hand often gripped protectively in Bill's. On the surface at least my brother seemed the golden boy – a handsome, talented, humorous man at the height of his powers. Yet there was also a sadness about him sometimes, a sort of restless anxiety. I saw no obvious reason why. Occasionally my mother or father would comment on it too, speculating as to whether Bill was secretly pining for parenthood. It was true that Bill would sometimes talk of the spare room where his wife spent her afternoons painting as 'junior's nursery', but then he would dismiss the subject, or quickly turn it into a joke.

One sultry afternoon in late August, sometime around 1984, I visited Ruth at the flat in Wandsworth where they were then living. My sister-in-law was working on a silk screen print she was making as a gift for a friend. While we were talking, Bill returned home from the office.

He looked tired and stressed as he walked through the door, his face, although smiling, almost grey with exhaustion, his eyes too prominent, the skin beneath them stretched taut by lack of sleep. Slumping into a chair, he pulled off his tie and poured himself a glass of wine. After chatting for a while, he then went into the other room, picked up the headset from the stereo, and with an Elmore Leonard crime novel in one hand and a joint in the other, proceeded to 'get out of it' the only way my brother knew how.

We sat like that for a while afterwards, Ruth working quietly and occasionally addressing the odd remark in my direction, apparently resigned to her husband's homecoming ritual of mind-numbing behaviour. I glanced at the title on the cover of the novel Bill was so gripped by. It was called *The Hunted*, the short blurb summarising the tale of a man, Al, being pursued by Motor City mobsters. A single quote stood out and caught my attention: 'The guys he's been hiding from know exactly where he is. And they're coming to get him – crooked lawyers, men with guns and money, assorted members of the mob who are harbouring a serious grudge.'

I smiled. Like many of his generation, Bill loved fantasies of guns and gangsters. When we were children it had been westerns that fired him up, got him excitedly tussling with me, the solitary squaw, even after the television was long switched off. My mother had worried that Bill was too easily influenced by such dramas, his boundaries blurred between reality and fiction.

Out in the kitchen making coffee, Ruth suddenly sighed. 'I wish Bill would get interested in something,' she said to me. 'I know he's tired after work. But this using a drink and a joint to retreat into a cocoon can't be good. I don't like what coke does to him either . . .'

This was the first time Ruth had mentioned Bill's 'social use' of cocaine. She told me it was usually provided at dinner parties by the same old schoolfriend who, having now served his time for dealing in cannabis, had come out of prison to promptly start dabbling in the stuff. Ruth instinctively disliked him, and wanted him out of her husband's life – but Bill would not drop him.

Ruth described in detail the effect that taking cocaine had on Bill, how suddenly aggressive and alienated he could become, and how much she would like him to find some form of creative engagement which was not just work.

Other journalists might numb themselves with too much booze, but some of them at least returned from the wars to find something a little more engaging than cocaine and gangster fiction. Something more was missing. Bill's peer group of college friends and work colleagues meanwhile were beginning to have children, as had I.

My own nappy-strewn condition, however downtrodden a twenty-five-year-old mother of two might have appeared, seemed to make Bill's sadness worse. With no children himself, and with no apparent intention of having any, nothing in our lives ever divided us as much. He could not understand it – the rocklike impenetrability of my motherhood. Far more effectively than any male rival, my children from now on blocked our previous intimacy.

Our fundamental affection, however, had not paled. Bill encouraged me to start pursuing a career in journalism myself, boosting my post-baby lack of confidence and showing immense pride in my achievements as my first features began to appear in women's magazines such as *Cosmo* and *Marie Claire*.

But as far as Bill was concerned, I was still the 'carer', the mother at the school-gates and the one who would, at the end, have to look after our increasingly frail parents. This crisis was not long in coming. Our mother, who suffered from osteoarthritis, had known for some time that she would need to go into hospital for a hip replacement. As my father came from a generation of Irishmen almost incapable of domesticity of any kind, she had kept postponing it. But now that her mobility was becoming more noticeably affected, Bill and I agreed to share looking after my father in her absence in hospital.

I volunteered to go over each morning, after dropping off our daughters at school, to my parents' house in Clapham, a fifteen-minute drive from our own small Victorian terrace in Wandsworth. Bill agreed to call in on my father each day after work, occasionally staying overnight if he was on a late shift. Except that it didn't work out like that. According to my father, Bill's comings and goings were increasingly random.

Arriving at my parents' house one morning, I found that Bill had spent the previous night there, sleeping in his old room next to my parents' room. My father was hinting heavily, although obviously reluctant to betray his son's confidence, that all was not well in Bill's and Ruth's marriage.

On going upstairs to make my father's bed, I found Bill's room resembling a tableau from the *Rake's Progress*: an empty bottle left carelessly on the floor, dribbles of red wine creating a bloody trail across the blue carpet. What had once been a starched Egyptian cotton sheet was now a damp, limp rag of indeterminate colour. The room stank too – of sweat, smoke and overnight acrid male anxiety. Whatever Bill was up to, it was not good. The atmosphere in the room was one of chaos, emotional rather than functional, its untidiness a symptom more of my brother's mental disturbance than his indolence.

Much later Bill himself wrote the story in a rare (for him) piece of confessional journalism published much later in *The Times* – a feature on infidelity inspired by, of all things, the 'highly public affair' of the television presenter Anthea Turner that was then dominating the headlines.

'For almost ten years of marriage, my wife had shown me nothing but love, tenderness and care,' Bill's account began. 'She was gentle and sweet-natured, not suspecting for a moment that her husband could betray her.' But he could and he had – admitting in the article, published in April 1998, that he had betrayed Ruth several times while on 'foreign assignments for the BBC'.

'None of these discreet dalliances ever came to light,' he wrote. 'I meant nothing to those I had slept with and they meant nothing to me – my marriage was safe, I loved my wife and she loved me.

'We were both in our early thirties, I had a good salary and I wanted children. She was not so sure about a family, so we delayed making a decision until it was too late.

'It is easy to slip into serial philandering, and once on that path of secret betrayal it is almost inevitable that it turns your life upside down.' That is indeed what happened to Bill.

'I met "Jane" – not her real name – while following politicians during the election campaign of 1987,' the story continued, 'six gruelling weeks on the road that threw us together almost every day. Within a fortnight we were sleeping together.' Bill had told the woman that his own marriage was effectively over and they were now apart.

'At first, my wife suspected nothing. She accepted excuses that I could not return at the weekend, merely expressing sadness that she had seen so little of me . . . When I eventually plucked up the courage to tell her the truth, she was devastated.'

In fact, it wasn't quite like that. I remembered very clearly what Bill himself had told me at the time about the way Ruth discovered that he was having an affair. How she found out was particularly cruel. It was a late evening in the summer of 1987 and they were both due to leave the following morning on a touring holiday in south-west France. My sister-in-law was still busy packing when the telephone suddenly rang.

It was around midnight. Bill was out, supposedly on a late shift at the BBC. He described to me afterwards, in various tense instalments, what Ruth had told him of that horrible phone call when he finally got home. A man's voice had asked for 'Mrs Frost'. He told her: 'I think you should know. Your husband is having an affair.'

Bill got home to find Ruth, shocked, angry, and very, very wounded. Bill admitted the relationship. He explained that he had met this woman while travelling together on the Tory campaign trail for the 1987 election. He assured Ruth, as indeed he himself now seemed to believe, that the affair was over. After staying up half the night arguing, he persuaded her that they should still go away as planned. God knows why – but Ruth agreed.

It was not a dream holiday. They drove across France to Blaye on the mouth of the Gironde, a beautiful old town Ruth had known as a student. Ruth's bottle-green MG Midget promptly broke down as if in sympathy with its owner's distress. Abandoning the car to be later towed back by the AA, they travelled back to England together, according to my brother, in mutual silent misery.

There now followed – not only for Bill and Ruth, but also for their families and friends – a period of unhappy bewilderment. Ruth was intelligent, cultured, sensitive and above all deeply loyal. It simply did not seem possible to her that Bill could have ceased loving her. My mother, when Ruth came to visit her in hospital where she was still recovering from her hip operation, was appalled by the ravaged transformation she saw in her daughter-in-law. In the space of only a few weeks, Ruth had lost nearly 2 stone in weight and her eyes were smudged with dark rings.

'How could he? How could he?' was all my mother would say, referring not to his infidelity, which she could have forgiven, but to his lies and deceit.

Ruth's own parents had their own more straightforward view of their son-in-law's betrayal, and Ruth's mother wrote Bill an apocalyptic letter in which she hoped 'that he would burn in the fires of hell' for what he had done to her daughter. My brother never forgot the curse, and later in his life, when mentally addled by drugs and alcohol, was to recall it in abject terror. Full of remorse, he now begged Ruth for forgiveness, claiming that his affair had been a one-off sexual distraction. Bill was baffled by Ruth's understandable fixation on the minutiae of his infidelity, dwelling on the details of a particular lie, an evening he had spent with this woman rather than her, and a bottle of perfume, Chanel, instead of Worth, showing on his credit card.

Any woman could have told Bill that this was a natural reaction for a deceived wife. But he genuinely could not see how, once he had decided to forget the affair, Ruth couldn't obligingly do the same. But she could not. Bill's initial pleas for reconciliation turned into macho posturing – booze and drugs to drown out the recriminations, and more booze and drugs to obliterate the guilt. 'I just need to get out of it,' he would answer my scolding. 'Wouldn't anyone?'

After a horrible few weeks, Ruth went away on an extended trip to California – both to see old friends, and to do what she could to repair what remained of her heart.

Now it was Bill's turn to feel afraid. Terrified that he might have lost her for ever, he wrote long and passionate letters to his betrayed partner. He wrote in his article: 'A friend showed me photographs. At first, I did not recognise the woman I married – always petite and very attractive, she now looked stunningly sophisticated too. I bombarded her with letters and, when I felt brave enough, long phone calls. She was cool and distant, but who could blame her?

'I told her I wanted to put the marriage back together,' Bill wrote. 'That I had indeed changed my ways and the relationship with Jane was over. She asked me whom I was seeing now – "after all, you are incapable of being on your own".' Ruth of course was absolutely right; Bill could not stand being alone. In her absence he stayed both at our parents' home and with his former Dulwich schoolfriend, Richard Hearn, and his girlfriend, Beverley Byrne, in their house on Streatham Common.

When, after six weeks away in America, Ruth arrived back in London she looked tanned, well-dressed and glamorous. She also seemed in a far fitter frame of mind to deal with her deceitful husband.

Dropping Ruth off at the flat where Bill was nervously awaiting her, Bev witnessed them 'falling into one another's arms'. She left convinced that Bill's affair had been a temporary aberration in an otherwise serene marriage. But Bev's instincts were wrong. Over the next three months, Bill's and Ruth's remade relationship very publicly fell to pieces.

The certainties of our childhood were also starting to crumble. Quite suddenly, following a hospital admittance for a minor routine prostate operation, our father became seriously ill. Within only a few weeks, bronchitis had turned into pneumonia. If Bill, as he himself admitted in his confessional diary, 'needed any further excuse, any bogus justification to increase my alcohol intake and behave promiscuously, my father's death provided it'.

Cruelly exploiting his wife's forgiveness, Bill had set out to make himself so impossible to live with that Ruth would eventually become the one to leave him. Although, and to Ruth's eternal credit, she supported my brother through those early months of visceral bereavement, Bill's only response was further betrayal – a brief affair with a work colleague from the BBC. The outcome was inevitable. Bill himself recorded in his article:

'The prelude to our final parting was played out at a party in North London given by mutual friends who were determined we would stay together against the odds. All went well until I struck up a conversation with a woman waiting to use the bathroom. It was entirely innocuous – a suggestion our hosts should install a second lavatory before throwing a party for so many guests again. She laughed at this none too witty bon mot and we chatted.

'Moments later my wife was between us, her eyes blazing with fury. "He is my husband, for what that's worth. Get your own man!" she screamed. There was an appalling silence before the guest assured my wife "she had no interest in me whatsoever". We left shortly afterwards and rowed all the way home.

'To all intents and purposes, that was the last night of our marriage. The next Monday I was posted to South Africa for six months and my wife decided she would stay in London. "Why travel to Johannesburg to be unhappy there?" she said, summing up the marriage succinctly. "At least I have friends and family here; there is nothing for me if I come with you."

'In the event, she did join me towards the end of my stay. For a few weeks it seemed there might be something to build on but the suffering she had already endured was too great. We parted soon after I returned to London and divorced two years later. I have not heard from her since . . .'

Ruth had gone from his life but, as she had so accurately predicted, her place was already being filled by another – the woman Bill had first encountered on the Thatcher campaign trail, and the 'Jane' of his confessional story. Her name was Barbara Jones – a journalist.

6

I had heard much about Bill's new girlfriend before meeting her.
Arriving at my mother's one evening with our twin daughters,
Katy and Maria, by then aged ten, Christy and I entered the
garden via the double wooden doors in front of the detached
garage. There on the carport was Bill's car, a woman's clothes
suspended on a hanger between the seats.

As we peered curiously inside I saw a Black Watch tartan
pleated skirt with matching waistcoat, and a cream blouse with a
rounded Peter Pan collar. I knew at once that they did not belong
to my sister-in-law Ruth. Christy and I looked at one another.
These clothes could only belong to Bill's new lover, Barbara. She
must be here at my mother's house right now.

Apprehensively we walked in. It was going to be a difficult
meeting. Ruth was not only my sister-in-law, she was my friend. Yet
my first loyalty lay with Bill, my brother, even when he had
betrayed his wife. I hoped Ruth could forgive me.

I returned Barbara's smile as Bill introduced us. 'Hello,' I said.
'I've heard so much about you,' meaning from Bill. 'Me, too,' she
replied smiling, 'Bill talks about you a lot.'

Barbara Jones was a strong woman who provoked extreme
reactions in the opposite sex. Having brought up her two sons
single-handedly, she had learned how to survive. She had carved
out a flamboyant career as a tabloid journalist, with a string of
professional admirers and jealous rivals left along the way. She
was by then in her early forties and, like Ruth, older than Bill by
several years.

Pale-skinned and attractive, with well-cut, short, straight

blonde hair, Barbara possessed an unusual and overwhelming self-confidence. She was also adept at flattery, particularly in the presence of men, and had a disarming but journalistically very useful ability when talking to someone to make them feel as if they were the most important person in the world – as she clearly made Bill feel.

He seemed completely obsessed with her. She in return could be overwhelmingly kind and devastatingly crushing all at once. It was as if, I supposed, he had met someone with a personality powerful enough to match his own. It was a question of who would break first.

Barbara hunted foxes, and any objections Bill might have had were swept away by her enthusiasm. She not only made sure my brother learned to ride, but also made him a present of a magnificent horse named Churchill, to whose care – every weekend at her cottage in Wiltshire – she seemed dedicated. The idea of Bill on a horse seemed ludicrous to me.

Men, she was later to tell me, were like dogs and horses, needing to have their spirit broken before they could be trained to obey. In Bill it seemed she had met a suitable challenge. I was amazed at the ease with which Barbara at first appeared to 'manage' my brother. Being 'handled firmly' was either what he wanted or needed. Gone was his normal headstrong egotism and in its place was an almost emasculated obedience.

His friend Pat Bishop noticed: 'Bill's basic conservatism was attracted to certain aspects of Barbara's life. Hunting with hounds, and skiing holidays – these rituals seemed an incongruous mix with Bill's personality, but he obviously came to enjoy them.'

When marriages break up, people take sides. Ruth had been held in deep affection by Bill's oldest friends, as by me. His cruel treatment of her had been played out all too publicly. If Bill was a still-just-about-lovable rogue, they refused to warm to his new consort Barbara. His university friends one by one fell away – back into their seemingly neatly ordered lives.

But sisters cannot choose – Bill and I had had a sibling pact since our teens that we always came first for one another. Partners might be transitory, but our loyalty to one another was immutable. I had loved Ruth, but I could not reject this new woman in Bill's life without running the risk of also losing him. Nor could I deny that Barbara Jones was 'good' for him. Everything she did was tackled with bustling energy and enthusiasm for life – her journalism, her children, her garden, her horses, her lover. Where Bill once might have been slumped on a sofa, joint in hand, he was now mucking out stables or striding up Silbury Hill.

Barbara's country cottage was suitably remote from Bill's seamier urban pursuits, although Bill kept the flat in Wandsworth, with Barbara providing the money to discreetly buy out the scorned wife's marital share. Barbara had insisted on redecoration. Pictures of hares being pursued by snarling dogs quickly replaced Ruth's serene oriental landscapes on the walls. Metronoming between London and the West Country began a pattern in Bill's life of perpetual motion, usually on a motorway somewhere between a girlfriend's house and work.

Throughout this time Bill remained a socially heavy drinker, but seemed restrained (at least in her company) from taking drugs by Barbara's intense disapproval. As he later recorded in his Priory confessional: 'By now I was living with a fellow journalist who did not mind my drinking, but took a dim view of coke – we argued about my drug use all the time.'

There were plenty of arguments, and not just about Bill's drug-use. He seemed to be eaten up by a deepening and almost pathological jealousy that made him vulnerable to the slightest nuance of Barbara's voice, look or touch. The paranoia reached such extremes of absurdity that he once telephoned me to say he was convinced Barbara was 'fucking the decorator' who was repainting the flat.

The rows became even more toxic. Restaurants and parties were free-fire zones – any startled onlooker being required to adjudicate who was right and who was wrong. After the last insult had been thrown, Barbara would simply depart for the country, with Bill compulsively driving after her, prompting the whole exhausting cycle of slamming doors and revving cars to start all over again.

In the midst of all the craziness, there was love. Bill and

Barbara collaborated on various journalistic projects – and she flattered and reinforced his belief, if not perhaps in the integrity of his personality, in his talent. She was also hugely kind to me, making connections and opening doors to push along my own career as I now became a writer for the *Daily Mail.*

And if Barbara and I were united, it was not in wanting to slap Bill down, but to rescue him. He was behaving badly, I have to admit. He seemed to want to get drunk as quickly as possible, before beginning scatological rants and insulting Barbara's harmless-enough country friends. Sometimes it was a party-trick, as if Bill were a performing seal expected to enliven with his antics an otherwise stodgy affair. Sometimes it could be hilarious. Most times, though, it was just not funny at all.

There was a big change coming, one that Barbara massaged from the sidelines. Bill's restlessness had turned into now ritualised expressions of frustration with his job at the *Today* programme. He did not get on with his new female boss and, blocked in an ambition to move into television, he was increasingly dissatisfied.

He was thus flattered and intrigued when Alan Copps, an executive at *The Times*, approached him, after the two shared a press trip on a royal tour to Belize in 1989, to move from radio into newspapers. Alan recalled: 'Simon Jenkins, the editor, had asked me to seek out new talent. Bill's personality was perfect for radio, but he said that he was starting to feel limited. I thought he would be perfect for us . . .'

Bill joined as chief reporter in October 1990. His first assignment was the Gulf War, where he was one of a team 'scattered across the sandpit', as he himself put it. Bill was based at Incirlik in south-eastern Turkey, frustratingly marooned near the perimeter of a US airbase, watching – from a broken-down hotel inhabited only, it seemed, by hard-drinking journalists – bombers take off and return.

Bill's friend and colleague at *The Times*, Danny McGrory, who was in Incirlik with him, remembers Bill's amazing ability to produce wonderful prose, even when under the most pressured of circumstances, and also his innate love of mischief:

'One night we were in a bar where the entertainment was a group of bellydancers. Around them was a group of dirt-poor children, all trying to sell flowers to the audience for them to throw to the girls.

'Several children approached one table where an ostenta-tiously showy and disgustingly fat man was sitting, surrounded by fawning cronies. Disdainfully, he offered the children a few coins.

'Bill saw their humiliation and, generously pulling out wads of notes, called the children over and told them he wanted to buy all the flowers they had. Amazed and grateful, the children grabbed the money, handing over the flowers to Bill, who proceeded to hurl bunch after bunch at the stage until the place was in chaos.'

Neither the switch from radio to print journalism, nor Bill's absence at the wars, improved his relationship with Barbara Jones. They could still tolerate each other's company – just about. Barbara meanwhile had a new project, a new way of 'sort-ing Bill out'. The former marital flat was sold at her insistence and a new house was found: No. 6 Wiseton Road, Wandsworth, just a few streets away from my own home.

Our mother now lived alone, frail and vulnerable to frequent burglaries, in the house a mile or so away in Clapham Park where we had grown up. That too was briskly put on the market, and sold to part-purchase the new house where it seemed the three of them – Mum, Bill and Barbara – were to live. Mum moved into the new ménage looking utterly bewildered. How was this strange arrangement meant to work? Bill was a front-line newspaper reporter, not a self-sacrificing carer.

Then Yugoslavia fell apart. Bill had a new arena of suffering in which he might drown his own.

7

Bill was among the very first wave of journalists to see the savage new conflict in the Balkans. He got to Belgrade, the Yugoslav capital, in the autumn of 1991 when the rumbling civil war was barely being reported in the British press. In November he was in Vukovar, the Croat town on the banks of the Danube which two days earlier had been smashed to pieces by Serb forces. In a ruined hospital he found:

'The basement ward where the last of the wounded are being treated is dark, dirty and malodorous. The floor is littered with bloody dressings. Doctors, nurses and orderlies look as dazed and shell-shocked as those they are treating. An old woman with wild hair cried out to go home. The nurse changing her bandages said: "Quiet, mother, your home is gone."

'Tucked away in the corner of the ward were wounded waiting to die. Every so often a nurse or doctor would clutch a hand and smile reassuringly at a patient with the glazed expression that precedes the death rattle. The Serb-led forces were yesterday determined to convince the outside world that the Croat defenders of Vukovar carried out atrocities before most of them fled the town. Positive proof had been promised that 40 children were murdered before the fall of Vukovar.'

In the summer of 1992 Bill was back there – this time in Sarajevo, then under siege from Serb artillery and snipers. On one occasion Bill came under fire, running, falling and badly injuring his leg.

After hospital treatment in London (keyhole surgery on his knee), Bill insisted on returning to the Balkans, this time to the winter mountains of central Bosnia where the British army had arrived under a UN mandate to protect aid convoys. He was in and out of Bosnia until the following spring, reporting on the horrors of 'ethnic cleansing' with passion and precision. On breaks home in London, he told me some of it himself: the story of the destroyed village, the men nailed to their burned-out houses. How did he stand it?

One way he coped was by drinking. I could see that for myself. But there was more than that, a lot more. After my brother's death I discovered this extraordinary piece of confessional that Bill had written in the Priory: 'The siege of Vukovar was perhaps the most brutal fighting I had ever seen. The town was shelled night and day – hospitals and schools were flattened, civilians who ventured from their cellars were picked off by snipers.

'It was gross and I began self-medicating with slivovitz, the local spirit. I began with a tumbler first thing in the morning. All the while my consumption was rising and during the siege of Sarajevo I discovered opium tea. Unfortunately the drug makes you dream and it was in Sarajevo that my nightmares began.

'Thirteen times I went to the former Yugoslavia. I saw murder, torture and massacre. The images of blood and atrocity are too vivid for me to mention or share. And needless to say I self-medicated in them all.'

That was his expression for it. Like the cocaine from the 'bent pharmacist' in Beirut, like the opium tea in Sarajevo, dosing himself up was becoming the only way he could operate in the wars. And soon it would become the only way he could operate away from them.

Another way of surviving was humour. Bill could be very funny, even if his jokes were increasingly black. Pat Bishop remembers: 'Bill, Victoria Clark of the *Observer* and I were driving around in an armoured van together, and although under the most stressful conditions imaginable, thanks to Bill we spent a lot of the time laughing.'

Emma Wilkins, Bill's colleague at *The Times*, summed up the contrast between his cool professionalism and the blundering mess he made of his personal life: 'His ability to craft a fine phrase placed him head and shoulders above most of his colleagues,' she said. 'His talent seemed to come so effortlessly. Yet in more mundane areas of life, he seemed to just find things so very difficult.'

Back in England meanwhile it was, by now, not just difficult, but downright impossible for Bill and Barbara Jones to maintain their relationship. He found it, so he told me later, far more emotionally demanding than any foreign battlefield. The horse-riding days were long over. When not actually working, he was behaving as he had done with Ruth, slumping with a joint and a bottle of wine. Barbara was running out of patience. Bill's jokes had stopped making her laugh long ago. The public rows were less frequent as they were hardly ever in public together. When they were, they seemed unable to be in each other's company for half an hour without some bizarre new explosion.

8

At the beginning of March 1994, we were suddenly propelled into serial family death. Returning from a Sunday drive, we were met at the front door by our two teenage daughters, Maria and Katy, both looking shocked and tearful. While Christy and I had been out, they had received a telephone call from their grandmother. Christy's father, Flann, who had by then retired to his native Ireland and had recently celebrated his seventy-fifth birthday, had suffered a heart attack and died instantly. A week later I was away in Leeds, working on an interview, when my aunt, my mother's twin sister, also died suddenly.

Three weeks later, and almost certainly as the result of delayed shock, my mother herself suffered a massive ischaemic stroke, surviving her sister by only a few weeks.

The loss of our mother, although hard enough for me, seemed almost to threaten Bill's ability to function at all. There had always existed between mother and son an intense dependency that was never resolved.

Together Bill and I organised the funeral, supporting one another through the ghastly unctuousness of the Streatham undertaker, alternately giggling and weeping over a whisky in the bleak pub afterwards.

But over the months that followed I became increasingly worried about Bill's state of mind, as did many of his close friends and colleagues. One evening at a party to celebrate the fortieth birthday of a journalist friend, I was abruptly approached by the executive editor of *The Times*. Launching straight into expressing both his enormous respect and liking for my brother, he also voiced his recent concerns:

'Not that Bill's work is suffering. But he appears to be so distressed since the death of your mother. He is an extremely talented man and I personally would do anything for him, anything at all. He only has to say the word, you know. Tell him that from me, if you don't think he would be too embarrassed.'

He was right, I knew. Bill clearly was not coping with his grief, drinking heavily, often alone, as well as arguing more – if that were possible – with Barbara. Although I did tell Bill what his boss had said, he did not appear to take it in. His only worry was whether there had been even the merest suggestion of criticism of his performance at the paper. He waved the conversation away as little more than party gossip.

That autumn, Bill and Barbara finally separated. Bill himself had described the end of the affair in his uncharacteristically self-revelatory *Times* article: 'For a while, we were happy. Then our own mutual distrust of each other began to sour the relationship,' he wrote. 'I accused her of infidelity and she laid the same charges against me.'

'Inevitably,' wrote Bill, 'we split up amid recriminations and squabbling over property.'

This time there was to be no passionate reconciliation. An intimacy remained, however, and Bill's 'friendship' for Barbara, and hers for him, never evaporated. Away from Bill, in her talks to me, Barbara remained affectionate and concerned. There we were, the two of us, the sister and the de facto estranged wife, both loving in our own way this talented, self-destructive child – and wondering what the hell to do. She saw disaster coming long before I did.

He was too good to just let go to the devil. Barbara would continue to believe that – and, more to the point, try and do something about it – right until the very end. And for that I am hugely grateful.

Our mother was dead. Bill's relationship with Barbara Jones was over. I had my own deep concerns with increasingly difficult teenage daughters. Bill's antics and upheavals were just too exhausting – too tedious for me to offer more than a long-range counselling service. But I sensed that terror of loneliness in him, that craving for the comfort of women which I as his sister could only provide in carefully controlled doses. 'Look Bill,' I would say, 'sort yourself out, you know how attractive you are. Just be nice, be your real self. Don't drink so much. You'll find somebody . . .' He did.

About two months after the final break-up with Barbara, I met Bill one night in the local wine bar after work. He suddenly produced his cheque book from his pocket, indicating a number and name scribbled on the cover in black biro. I looked down and read it – 'Alex Hanley'. Bill told me he had briefly known Alex about ten years before. He and Ruth had once been to a party at her house. She was married then and lived in a very grand house with shutters in the Holland Park end of Notting Hill. Now she was single again, mother to Louis, then in his late teens, and his half-brother Max, a severely handicapped ten-year-old.

Bill confided how much he had been attracted to Alex in the past, and that having met up with her a few nights earlier at a gallery opening in Chelsea, he would like to ask her out. I asked him what was stopping him.

I still remember clearly the brief and, with hindsight, now loaded conversation that followed. Bill told me that Alex's family were 'a bunch of south London characters – entertaining, but probably better not to become involved with'.

I responded immediately, 'Well, just take her to a film or something. You don't have to fall in love with her.'

PART TWO

9

Bill had only been seeing Alex Hanley for a few weeks when he first announced that he would like us to meet her. It seemed especially important, I supposed, that with few surviving relatives, introducing Alex to me and my family was the closest he could come to asking her to 'meet the parents'.

We met in a wine bar just a few streets away from both our houses. It was autumn 1994 and the first glimpse I had of Alex was of a tall blonde in her late forties, dressed smartly in a grey polo neck, navy blue Joseph jacket and narrow blue denims. There was an air of fragility, of damage, about her – Marianne Faithfull, but not quite so resilient.

She smiled hesitantly at Christy and me as we walked forward to introduce ourselves, her unusually pale blue eyes blinking rapidly, and appearing slightly unfocused as she looked up. I could see immediately why she would appeal to Bill who, although now himself in his early forties, remained an admiring acolyte of the Rolling Stones, and Mick Jagger in particular.

Glancing over at Bill affectionately as we talked, Alex seemed in need both of security and reassurance from him. Her voice, husky and nervously breathless, broke a little as she described the condition of her youngest son, Max, who suffered cerebral palsy as a result of a genetic defect, as well as frequent epileptic fits. She had been divorced twice, so Bill would tell me.

Alex struck me as vulnerable, and more than slightly tragic. But sitting cosily chatting with my brother and his new girlfriend, I did not pick up on anything that should have given cause for alarm. As any mother would, I felt tremendous sympathy for her and could only imagine how difficult life must be as a single woman coping with such a severely handicapped child.

At the same time, I had my doubts about whether it was a good idea for Bill to become so involved with her, as he obviously was, quite so quickly. I wondered whether never having had any children of his own, he was capable of the patience and selflessness that would be required of him as the surrogate father to Alex's disabled son.

Alex told us that Max's father was now living in Dubai with his new partner, also a journalist. The couple had since had a baby daughter of their own, but had Max to stay with them for several weeks each year.

She was very frank about the cause of her son's disability, which had been genetically traced to her side of the family. Her brothers had been lucky as it seemed they did not carry the defective gene. Alex did.

It was a tragic, awful story. Yet Alex herself appeared courageously optimistic about her son's future, describing to me how she was taking him to one specialist or another, determined to make the best she could of both their lives.

When not discussing Max, Alex showed a far lighter side, a flaky butterfly of a woman, dizzily hurtling from one airhead topic to another, while frequently throwing the names of her many female friends into the shallow stream of conversation which flowed at me rather than between us for the rest of the evening.

Although the evening bubbled brightly with the latest doings of her celebrity friends, I felt Alex was not so much boasting as desperately seeking common ground. I came away thinking that, although I could not understand what Bill found so magnetic about Alex Hanley, she seemed likeable enough. Here was another possibility of love, perhaps another go at life itself. No harm in that.

Over the next few months, Bill's relationship with Alex intensified rapidly. Knowing his capacity for such fiery all-consuming affairs, I tried to caution him to take things slowly. Alex, perhaps as a result of being abandoned in the past, was more wary of commitment than Bill. My brother was aware of her need for distance, but it just made him both more insecure and more persistent.

It was coming back, I could begin to sense it – Bill's inner rage of seething jealousy, which later and disastrously was to be directed against the one person who undeniably had the right of first-call on Alex: her son, Max.

At Bill's insistence, Alex moved into Wiseton Road. At first the relationship seemed contented and far less turbulent than that with Barbara. Bill was calmer. The number of his calls to me, always a key indicator of his mood, dropped dramatically. Only his habitual phone call on his arrival at his desk at *The Times*, a reassurance check and throwback to the days when our parents were alive (he had the same habit of ringing them), remained as constant as ever.

When we did talk for longer – or meet up – he described their time spent together. It seemed to be one long party. Alex had many friends, nearly all women; and apart from looking after Max at weekends, networking with them took priority in her life and, sometimes to his extreme annoyance, over Bill. It was easy to see why. Having survived two broken marriages, she had learnt to value these female alliances more highly than the potentially transitory presence of a man. Nevertheless, Bill put up with her female friends for now. He was obviously in love with the idea, if not the reality, of Alex Hanley.

But he could not pick and choose the package to suit his needs. Having Alex meant accepting Louis, and Max too, not just for weekends or the odd evening's babysitting, but for life. Bill could never really accept it and somehow convinced himself that he and Alex might one day be alone. Even more delusionally, he also seemed convinced that he and she might have their own children. This was beyond even Bill's talent for getting what he wanted, given Alex's understandable reluctance to have another child. With a total, toddler-like conviction in his own omnipotence, Bill raged against anyone who dared to say otherwise.

Although he often declared to me that he would like children of his own, it was not to be. It always seemed to me that Bill must somehow deliberately have pursued women who for one reason or another were never likely to have children. His wife Ruth was not keen, and Barbara Jones had grown-up sons when Bill first embarked on his tempestuous affair with her. Perhaps he could not bear the idea of not being the sole focus of a woman's love. His friend and colleague at *The Times*, Alan Copps, recalled a discussion he had about fatherhood a few years before Bill's death. By then, Alan himself had three teenage children from his first marriage, but was now embarking on fatherhood again in his mid-forties:

'It was the most difficult and sensitive conversation I ever remember having with Bill,' Alan said. 'His childlessness was obviously an issue he felt very deeply about. I got the impression that this was a great sadness to him.'

On Christmas Eve 1994, about four months after Bill and Alex had begun seeing one another, I met Kevin Hanley and his wife, Lena, for the first time. Alex had invited Christy and me round to Wiseton Road for drinks to meet her youngest brother and his wife and two daughters, Olivia and Molly.

Friendly and humorous, as well as obviously doting on his two little daughters, then aged five and three, Kevin Hanley could have been any thirty-something Fulham father. He seemed charming, his daughters sweet and pretty, playing at his feet while his attractive blonde wife Lena, sitting on the arm of his chair as we talked, presented as a good Catholic wife and mother.

Lena's conversation was all about the children, their education and the school run. She seemed rather serious by comparison with both her husband and sister-in-law and, very much in the Irish tradition, definitely the dominant force in the family. The worst that could have been said of her was that she seemed rather bossy, used to having her instructions obeyed both by her husband and her children.

At the same time I was also introduced to Alex's and Kevin's mother, Bridget, another devout Catholic and a kind woman who, in spite of being then in her late sixties, frequently took care of Max. She clearly loved her grandson a great deal, and delighted in the smallest indication of any improvement in his condition.

I don't recall asking what Kevin did for a living. Bill had told me early in his relationship with Alex that the Hanley family had run a flower stall in the Fulham Road for several generations. I knew the one he meant, outside the Queen's Elm pub, having often driven by it. I assumed that Kevin was involved in organising and buying stock – wherever it was that cut flowers came from. All I knew was that, whatever it was that Kevin did, it seemed to involve being away from home rather a lot.

Later, during the spring and summer of the following year, I remember Lena frequently taking her girls to a caravan the family owned at a place called Pagham in West Sussex. If Bill was working, Alex would accompany her sister-in-law, taking Max and her mother along too. Occasionally Bill would join the others at the weekends, although always for some reason with reluctance. Although his obsession with Alex showed no sign of abating, he told me he loathed these visits to the 'caravan'. There was somewhere else, however, that he seemed to like better – staying with some wealthy couple Alex knew who owned a house with a swimming pool in the New Forest where they spent occasional weekends.

Although up in London for much of the time, Alex was also renting a cottage in Gloucestershire where Max attended a special school during the week. Bill, in a direct echo of his motorway-pounding existence with Barbara, was now having to get up early several mornings a week to drive to *The Times* newsroom in Wapping.

But early nights were not on the agenda. Their lives, whether in London or the country, seemed to consist of endless dinner parties with people I had never heard of, often continuing, according to Bill, well into the small hours. The partying was taking its toll. He looked permanently exhausted. His mood was changing, hardening. The infatuation with Alex was unbroken – but he seemed angry, not just occasionally at some perceived slight by his girlfriend or his bosses at work, but all the time. Very soon he would turn that anger on me.

Bill and I had scrapped like puppies in childhood. In spite of everything, we had rarely argued for more than a few hours in adulthood. There was a niggling issue, however. The sale of our mother's home had realised some money which should have come to me ages ago. It was still bound up in Bill's house and he seemed to have forgotten about it.

One morning I met my brother in the street as he was about to get into his car to drive to work. He looked gaunt and hollow-eyed. I asked him why.

'Oh . . . we had a dinner party last night, you know how it is . . . Alex's friends.' They hadn't gone to bed, he told me, until around four. He also said that he was worried about money, that he was spending a fortune, and was not sure whether he should sell the house in Wiseton Road and move out to the country.

I said I didn't think it was a good idea if it was only going to mean exhausting journeys to Wapping each day. I had worries of my own now. A sizeable proportion of my mother's estate was still locked up in Bill's house. If he did sell, I wanted my share out of the equation before any more of it evaporated. I had been used to Bill's temper all my life, but this was like nothing I had ever seen before. The transformation of his handsome if weary face into a mask of malignant hostility was like a demonic possession.

I don't know what he had taken the night before. Whoever it was now talking to me in that street bore no resemblance to the Bill I knew. Leaning over in a threatening manner, he released a stream of abuse, ranting about me, about Barbara, Alex and, it seemed, womankind in general: 'You're all bitches, the lot of you!'

There was nothing I could say or do to calm him. Instead, and in a gesture that seemed to anger him even further, I turned my back and walked away, leaving him to drive off in a rage.

For the rest of the morning I sat at home worrying about whether he had made it safely into work. Every now and again I dialled his extension at *The Times* only to find the line engaged. At lunchtime, to my relief, I at last received a call.

His voice sounded familiar again, the menacing edge I had heard that morning replaced by abject contrition: 'I'm so, so sorry . . . It was all my fault. I didn't mean any of it, really I didn't. I'm just so fucking tired . . .'

10

A month or two later I discovered I was pregnant with my third child. Although this was very much planned as far as Christy and I were concerned, my pregnancy came as a complete shock to the rest of the family, my brother included. With twin daughters now about to enter medical school, it had been assumed by everybody that our lives would now change focus, that we would become empty-nesters spending time together, as a colleague of Christy's at the *Telegraph* put it, 'touring France in search of ever swankier restaurants'. Instead, at the age of forty-two, I would yet again be staring into a nappy bucket.

But I didn't mind. It was what I wanted, and what we had both chosen. Bill's reaction was mixed, being both thrilled by the idea of becoming an uncle again, and at the same time deeply envious. He was still living life as the eternal naughty uncle, always with a woman but never a wife – or a mother to children of his own.

'It should have been mine,' was his saddest remark and the one that has remained with me ever since. My pregnancy symbolised for him both the stark difference in the choices we had made and the very separate ways our lives had developed. To Bill, my marriage represented a state of reassuring permanence, which he used according to his needs – either as a shrine to wonder at, or a shelter from the fall-out of his latest failed relationship. He would need that shelter all too soon.

It was New Year's Eve 1995 that I first began to get a really bad feeling about some of the visitors to his house. Bill and Alex were holding a party. Christy's elderly mother, Mary, was staying with us overnight, having made the trip from Dublin to see us.

I was one month pregnant, tired, as well as suffering from bouts of nausea, but I still wanted to see Bill and to go to the party. So we agreed that Christy, his mother and I would go round for a drink after we had finished supper, at around eleven o'clock.

I was very soon wishing I had not. From the moment I entered the house I began to feel I should not have come. As a small child in Brighton on holiday with my parents, I had once scared myself with an American horror comic, in which a woman wearing rose-tinted spectacles believes she is attending a glamorous cocktail party – only to discover as she removes her glasses that she is instead standing in the midst of a deserted graveyard surrounded by ghouls. It was coming true.

The front room was full of faces that looked as if they had been left in the water too long – mainly women in their late forties or early fifties, dressed indiscriminately in black or faded denim, all of whom seemed to answer to the name of Mandy. The air stank around us – a fetid fug of cannabis and high-tar cigarettes.

Their voices, inane cackling screeches, their pitch rising as the evening progressed, jarred on my ears like a poorly tuned radio. Suddenly I knew that both I and my unborn baby had to get out of there.

Fiercely I announced to Christy that he could stay if he liked, but I was leaving then and there. As the women around me began to commiserate patronisingly about the drawbacks of being pregnant, I remember thinking to myself, 'It's not that. It's all of you.'

To my great relief, Christy followed me home shortly afterwards, bizarrely abandoning his seventy-seven-year-old mother who was now enjoying herself hugely. Opting to remain, she finally ended up staying overnight at the party, apparently chatting away well into the small hours.

When we got home Christy and I sat – half laughing, half shaking – talking about the 'party'. He said he had also felt the horror-movie atmosphere of the house and its flaky guests. Afterwards I lay awake for several hours, unable to stop thinking about Bill. My mother-in-law appeared for a late breakfast, exclaiming excitedly and without condemnation: 'They're all druggies, you know . . .' She had always liked my brother.

Bill was by now in his mid-forties, far too old for all of this. Weren't people supposed to grow out of narcotics in the same way they grew out of acne and adolescent angst? There had been no real glamour, if such a thing exists, at the house in Wiseton Road that evening. Bill was not stuck in his own adolescence, he was stuck in other people's – who seemed not to know that the party was sometime supposed to end.

My son Joseph was born on 1 September 1996, three days before Bill's own forty-sixth birthday. On a soft September afternoon just a few hours after Joseph's birth, Bill rushed straight from the newsroom, overjoyed at the arrival of his nephew, to see me on the morning I came home. A new life, new hope, a new beginning.

Bill seemed happy enough too. Alex had come up with all sorts of distractions: trips to Spain, and a planned holiday in Florida with the whole Hanley family, where Max could swim with dolphins.

Bill could still speak movingly about Alex's handicapped son – how he played with him, fed him, washed him, carried him. In spite of the nature of Bill's pleasure-seeking, there still seemed a chance that caring for Max might anchor him in a sense of responsibility for someone other than himself. But it was not to be. Events had begun to unfold halfway across the world that were about to turn his life upside down.

The very day that Bill came to see my newborn son, an ocean-going trawler left the Caribbean island of Trinidad heading for a carefully planned rendezvous off the south coast of England. It was stuffed with cocaine. It was not the first such mission, nor, as I would discover, would it be the last.

Organising the trawler's reception was Kevin Stephen Hanley.

11

Bill the journalist would have liked the story of the *Sea Mist*. He would certainly have been attracted by the seamy glamour of its cast, and the self-congratulation of the bumbling forces of law enforcement. He would undoubtedly have made a number out of 'Dusty', the Irish customs sniffer-dog. But whatever he might have known at the time, Bill kept absolutely to himself. This was one story he was not going to report on. That would be left to me.

I would only be able to put together what happened four years after my brother's death. But what the Customs investigators revealed in our bleak meeting at the Treasury in January 2005 fitted exactly with what I knew of Bill's increasingly erratic behaviour in the summer and autumn of 1996. I had thought from what little he had told me at the time that he was living in fantasy-land. He was not.

It had begun with an accident of the weather. In late September 1996, a fishing boat was caught by a freak Atlantic storm off the coast of south-west Ireland. It was an unusual fishing boat. Built in Norway to face the toughest weather, big and powerful, its holds had been converted to make extra living-accommodation and to carry enough fuel to make ocean-spanning voyages. Crossing the Atlantic took twenty-five days.

There was engine trouble. The storm worsened. The *Sea Mist*'s skipper realised they would have to find shelter or the boat would founder. The trawler reached the entrance to Cork harbour in mid-afternoon, anchoring on Friday 27 September in open water off the sheltered fishing village of Aghada.

An observant yachtsman became suspicious. The new arrival,

clearly once a deep-sea trawler, carried no nets or fishing gear. No national flag was flying and the vessel's name seemed to have been crudely obscured. With the storm still raging, the anchorage near the mouth of Cork harbour, with its multiple channels and islands, was still dangerously exposed.

The snooping sailor went to the pierside pub to ask about the anonymous visitor. The landlady phoned the Gardai – the Irish police. The boat was kept under discreet observation throughout the next day. It moved further up the channel to anchor at East Ferry where a middle-aged man, a young woman and a small child were seen to go ashore.

Early on the morning of Sunday, the 29th, armed Gardai and a Customs officer went aboard. They found three men, who gave their names as 'Roman Smolen', 'James Noel' – both from St Lucia, Trinidad – and 'Howard Miller', of Ambleside in Cumbria, England.

It was engine trouble that had forced them into port according to a 'co-operative and helpful' Mr Smolen. They were on their way to Denmark to deliver the boat to a new owner, he explained, on behalf of its present owner, a 'Mr David Hunter', who had an address in the British Virgin Islands and was 'involved in the yacht charter business'. Once the storm had blown over, they would be on their way.

The Customs officers thought differently. Smolen was ordered to steer the boat to an enclosed former shipbuilding yard on Cobh island. On the bridge connected to a heavy-duty battery was a Motorola mobile phone. It rang during the move across the harbour. Smolen answered, telling the caller they were being taken in by the authorities.

The *Sea Mist* was ringed by armed police and naval personnel. 'Dusty' the sniffer dog came excitedly on board. He was especially interested in a spice rack above a cooker in the galley. Behind it were the sealed doors to a 'dumb-waiter', a lift running down to the galley. A crowbar was quickly summoned. Inside were hundreds of plastic bags of white powder. The hatch was re-sealed awaiting fingerprinting and forensics.

Overnight, meanwhile, the Gardai had raided an address on

Blarney Street in Cork City – to where they had followed the curious trio who had gone ashore from the *Sea Mist* the day before. They arrested a middle-aged man, identified from his passport as 'Gordon Richards' of Brighton, England. With him was a nineteen-year-old young woman identified as 'Theresa Bernadette da Silva Roy' of Puerto de la Cruz, Venezuela, plus a two-year-old boy named 'Edwin', who was evidently her son.

The *Sea Mist*'s rag-tag crew were placed in Cork's Bridewell prison. 'Edwin' was put in the care of social services. The ocean-going 'trawler' was taken apart.

Officers found sophisticated satellite navigation equipment, a logbook, nautical almanacs, maps and charts. They also found a parachute. Irish Customs discreetly contacted their British counterparts.

Forensic experts in Dublin meanwhile analysed the powder from the dumb-waiter and found it to be between 64 per cent and 85 per cent pure cocaine. Eventually a total of 599 kilos, with an estimated street value of £80 million, came out of the *Sea Mist*. The drugs were in three different kinds of packages wrapped in plastic tape. One of them had on the package a picture of the 'Ten of Diamonds' playing card.

At the subsequent court appearance, Gordon Richards pleaded guilty, but the others expressed complete innocence. Three months before the trip, the *Sea Mist*'s captain was approached by 'people who offered him money to go to Brest in France', or so Richards claimed in a pre-trial statement. He said he took his nineteen-year-old girlfriend and her son with him because he 'believed they were in danger'. Colombians and Venezuelans had threatened him, he claimed, and told him he 'would not live if he did not captain the trawler'.

They sailed from Puerto de la Cruz in Venezuela to the Caribbean island of Trinidad where the boat was repaired, Richards admitted – then 'an aeroplane dropped the shit off while we were at sea'. That explained the parachute. 'I knew it was contraband and was pretty sure it was cocaine,' said Richards. The fee for making the run, he admitted later, was $400,000.

The *Sea Mist* trial began in Cork in February 1997, and strict reporting restrictions were imposed until its conclusion. Theresa da Silva Roy, James Noel and Howard Miller claimed they had no knowledge that drugs were aboard. After two weeks of legal argument, the judge directed the charges against them to be dismissed.

Roman Smolen pleaded not guilty, and after a week-long trial the jury found the same. Leaving court, he praised Irish hospitality, telling reporters: 'I will continue to work as I have done. The sea is my life. I do not know anything else, but I will be careful not to get caught up in something like this again.' Gordon Richards was found guilty and sentenced to seventeen years for possession of cocaine with intent to supply.

The outcome of the *Sea Mist* trial was reported in Irish newspapers and in Irish editions of the *Daily Mirror*. It made minimal impact in the British press. Politicians and law enforcement officials in the Republic proclaimed a great victory in the war against drugs. What they did not admit, however, was that while over half a tonne of cocaine had been seized, at the end of the trial they had no idea who Richards had been working for.

Nor did the Irish authorities admit anywhere in public that, from very soon after the *Sea Mist* was impounded, undercover British Customs officers had been swarming all over the fishless trawler and its cargo of evidence looking for clues as to who might be running the British end of the operation. There was no mention of that in any subsequent press reports, nor would there ever be.

The phone on the bridge, the clunky Motorola '004' that had rung while the police were first aboard, was the key, so investigators indicated to me. From its SIM card and phone company records in London, the Customs discovered it was in the name of a British citizen, a middle-aged businessman and resident of Marbella, Spain, who owned several financial companies.

Records allegedly showed repeated calls between the 004 Motorola and a number ending '136' on the evening the *Sea Mist* diverted to Cork harbour. The 136 number was also registered to the Marbella businessman. A Venezuelan Airlines boarding pass was found on the *Sea Mist*, with a phone number scrawled on the back. It turned out to be that of Lymington Yacht Haven in Hampshire.

There was another scrap inscribed with the 136 number. A photocopy of an apparently genuine passport was also found – in the name of a forty-two-year-old American called 'Judith Parks'.

From the tide charts and a description of a sailing yacht found aboard, it became clear that before it was blown into Cork harbour, the *Sea Mist* was heading for the south coast of England, intending to rendezvous with a smaller boat a few miles offshore.

After the transfer of the drugs, the harmless-looking pleasure-craft would run innocently enough for harbour. The process was an old smuggler's trick known as 'coopering'. The South American end seemed impossible to penetrate, and ending up in Cork was a freak accident. There must be a British end, investigators assumed, in the affluent marinas and harbours of Hampshire and Dorset. It was a question of looking. Lymington Yacht Haven would do for a start.

In October 1998 Gordon Richards appealed from his Irish prison against the length of his sentence, but he was unsuccessful. His counsel argued: 'While it would appear that Richards was the nominal skipper of the ship, there was another person directing operations.' There most certainly was.

12

I had never heard of 'Brian Brendon Wright', nor had most people until the end of the Operation Extend trials in the summer of 2002 when reporting restrictions were at last lifted on the saga of crime and retribution that had begun with an Irish storm. According to the *Evening Standard*: 'The gang leader Brian Wright can be named today as Britain's most wanted drug smuggler. Wright escaped to Northern Cyprus which has no extradition treaty with Britain.'

But even if I had never heard of him, Mr Wright, a middle-aged, Irish-born 'entrepreneur', was very well known indeed in the racing fraternity as a high-rolling gambler with an uncanny knack of backing winning horses. It was the racing connection that would excite the media and the public much more than the drugs.

The BBC *Panorama* programme went big on that one. According to a special report broadcast in October 2002: 'Wright was betting sometimes £50,000 or £100,000 a time on [fixed] races. His best year was 1996. He rented a Thameside apartment in exclusive Chelsea Harbour, and bought a villa in Andalucia he called *El Lechero* – "The Milkman" – his nickname (earned for always delivering, or never going home until the early hours, depending on who you ask).'

Brian Brendon Wright had another nickname. On British racecourses he was also known as 'Uncle', at least by those jockeys on whom he showered hospitality. For years there had been rumours that 'Uncle Brian', with his celebrity friends, Ascot box and membership of Tramp nightclub in London, was the string-puller in a wave of alleged horse-doping and race-fixing scams stretching back to the 1980s.

Panorama held little back: 'Some jockeys enjoyed his cocaine. Others were supplied with prostitutes or brown envelopes stuffed with cash. One associate told us: "Sometimes when we put money on a race, we knew what was going to be first, second and third".'

But HM Customs & Excise had long suspected Brian Wright of being a drug importer. The gambling, the race-fixing – if that is what it was – was a convenient front for money-laundering.

It was the records from the *Sea Mist* phones, the Marbella connection, that alerted the Customs that the trawler's cargo might be destined for the still very shadowy 'Wright Organisation'. Concerted undercover surveillance began in April 1997. The Milkman rented a luxurious apartment at 19 King's Quay, Chelsea Harbour in west London, under the name 'D. Hood'. The rent of £2,000 a month was paid in cash.

The apartment was bugged. A telephoto lens caught an image of Wright staring out from his Thameside balcony. There were shadowy meetings in the nearby Conrad Hotel's long gallery. Names of associates began to emerge. A man in his late thirties seemed to be the Milkman's 'most trusted lieutenant'. His name was Kevin Stephen Hanley.

Customs began to pry into his affairs. Hanley lived in a substantial flat at the top of Putney Hill in south-west London, with his wife Lena and two young children. He also seemed to have a girlfriend called 'Anni'.

Anni Rowland would soon announce herself to be pregnant. Lena Hanley already was.

13

In that autumn and winter of 1996–7 Bill seemed more and more weighed down by some crushing anxiety. I had my own concerns – with a three-month-old baby – but I was prepared to listen. The partying and the rows with Alex continued unbroken, but this was something different. One morning he rang me from work telling me not to worry if I walked past his house and saw all the curtains drawn.

'Kevin is staying with me,' he said. 'He's in some . . . trouble. He needs to disappear for a few days.'

This was the language of pulp fiction. It was grandiose, juvenile – absurd. I asked Bill what sort of trouble Kevin was in. I imagined at best an argument with his wife, at worst some minor involvement with the police.

'He's been beaten up badly by some people – with baseball bats.' I was horrified. Yet Bill made it sound as if this was quite normal, something that occurred every now and again and that simply had to be got through.

'What, Bill? Why? This is appalling. Has Kevin been to hospital or told the police?'

Bill backtracked rapidly. 'No, yes, I mean . . . it's all under control . . . it's just a former mate of his, someone Kevin has fallen out with. Says Kevin owes him money.'

I put the phone down with sudden, gut-wrenching panic. I tried to remember all that Bill had told me about the Hanleys. He had talked of them jokingly as 'characters' when first describing Alex – lovable rogues, cheeky chappies, salt of the earth. What was this stuff about being beaten up with baseball bats?

Later that day I walked up Bill's street on the way to the bank. The curtains were indeed drawn tightly at every window, in a-don't-ask-what's-going-on-way, that seemed to me much more likely to draw attention than deflect it. I realised with a jolt that I too appeared to be entering into the darkening drama. Kevin was Alex's brother. Alex was Bill's girlfriend. Bill was my brother, so any friend of his was . . . what? A friend of mine?

I still had just enough cosy middle-class sentiment left to think it was all a mad fantasy. 'Why hadn't Kevin called the police immediately?' I asked my brother naively. There was no coherent answer. The only possible reason for not doing so, I told myself, was that Kevin was outside the law himself. The thought returned again to me – this man was still in my brother's house. I was suddenly very scared for Bill. What if Kevin's attackers should come back at night and try again?

There was another even crazier episode soon afterwards. Kevin's car, a black BMW estate, I think, had been 'ambushed' in Islington, north London, so Bill told me with alarmingly cool detachment. The way he said it – it was as if he'd had a puncture. Kevin had been driving along with cocaine hidden in the boot when two cars had suddenly pulled out of side streets on either side, heading Kevin off and simultaneously blocking his exit.

Kevin had at first thought it was 'a swoop by the police' – before recognising the men as 'Colombians' who had a grudge against him over some previous drug deal. He had 'fought them off', according to Bill, before somehow escaping.

Most people would have run away screaming from such people, but Bill right now seemed to be revelling in their company. I knew from past experience how easily my brother could be lured by the slightest whiff of sulphur – 'the devil always on one shoulder', as his friend Danny McGrory put it after his death. I remembered Bill's childhood friend Richard Hearn too recalling how Bill was always attracted by the kind of people 'it would be a laugh to have a drink with – but you'd be glad to walk away from by the end of the evening'. Up until now Bill had always walked away, making it back safely to familiar territory, his health and reputation just about intact. What absurd glamour attracted him to 'diamond geezer' Kevin Hanley?

I observed, or else heard about, the comings and goings at Wiseton Road over the next few months with an increasing unease. On one occasion I met Bill leaving his house in the company of an individual Bill introduced to me only as 'Barry'. Stubbily built and barrel-chested in an absurd Hawaiian shirt, a gold chain round his neck, next to my tall, chiselled brother in his Armani suit, they could not have looked more incongruous, a bizarre coupling of Bob Hoskins and Colin Farrell. They looked unlikely friends, and Bill seemed uncomfortable at being found in Barry's company. I got the impression that they had some urgent business to discuss, something they did not want to tell me and I certainly did not want to know.

Bill was then still in the habit of calling in to have a drink at our house almost every night on his way back from work. On a good evening Bill was entertaining, funny and affectionate. On a bad night, usually as a result of some ridiculous argument with Alex, he would be morose, gloom-laden and, as the months went on, increasingly agitated. Soon I would find out why.

A month or so after the meeting in the street with Barry, Christy and I had some building work done on our house which involved the installation of a new bathroom upstairs. There would be no hot water for weeks. With two fastidious teenage daughters as well as a small baby to wash, I called Bill at *The Times* to ask if we could borrow his bathroom while he was out at work. His reaction was odd, acting as though he wanted to help but at the same time as if I had presented him with an almost impossible request.

He told me that Alex was there and suggested it would be better for me to check with her first. I did ask Alex and she subsequently agreed, she did not seem any more comfortable with the idea than Bill had been.

Christy went round one day equipped with a key Bill had reluctantly provided in order to have a shave and a wash-down. He returned grinning broadly. The curtain-darkened house was untidy certainly, he told me, but the kitchen seemed full of the ordinary staples. A trail of clothes and discarded underwear led to the loft bedroom. The oddest thing was the bath itself, filled to the brim with lukewarm, cloudy water. A half-filled teacup perched on a saucer floated within, like a bloom on a lily pond. He had tested its contents: 'milk and two sugars'.

The next time our water was cut off, access to the Wiseton Road bathroom was denied. I went instead with our teenage daughters and Joseph to a family I knew who lived across the road from Bill. It was clear from Bill that whatever our sanitary predicaments, the bathroom in the darkened house, indeed any access, was now strictly off-limits.

A few weeks later I discovered why. It was about eleven o' clock on a slow Saturday morning, Christy semi-dressed and halfway through the weekend supplements, when Bill appeared unexpectedly on our doorstep, looking distinctly hunted – hands thrust deep into the pockets of his grey overcoat, his features stretched tight by fatigue.

Although he did his best to appear casual about his visit, accepting coffee and crouching down to play with Joseph on the floor, I sensed his agitation. He had left Alex and Max back at the house, he said. He had only called in to see us for a minute, just to get away from the morning chaos of getting Max bathed, dressed and breakfasted.

He tried to make a joke of it, but a sister's instinct told me that this was not why he had come. Something much more serious had happened. He said he had not slept much the night before and looked as if he had not even been to bed. Suddenly he blurted it out:

'There's a gun in the garden at Wiseton Road – a Smith and Wesson. I don't know what the fuck to do, but it's scared me rigid.'

I remember the sudden sweat of fear breaking out on my forehead as Bill spoke. I realised he was not joking.

'Get rid of it,' I said feebly. What I was saying was absurd – get rid of the gun buried in the flowerbed under the wisteria near where our mother used to sit on a sunny day. What I wanted to say – to scream at my brother – was get rid of Kevin Hanley too, even if it meant not seeing Alex ever again.

There was another change in Bill too. His skin was ageing. His eyes now were always ringed with dark smudges, his hair a shock of iron grey. That, and the perpetual runny nose. Christy could not stand it. It wasn't the evident cause he objected to so much, it was the bloody *sniffing*. Bill had always, always denied taking cocaine – had never offered it to me or taken a line in my presence. Now he was beginning to admit it outright, 'Every fucking journalist in London uses. You're so naïve,' he said angrily after I had gone for him harder than usual. I was indeed naïve – and far more so than I ever imagined.

But all this time, I was beginning to realise, Christy and I had slowly been drawn into accepting not just cocaine, but characters and events that seemed to have walked straight out of some second-rate crime drama. I had never met anyone like Kevin Hanley and his friends before, and having been introduced to them by Bill I had taken them on trust. But the arrival of a revolver into the plot was not something even my post-baby-blunted sensibilities could ignore. Bill's Wapping colleague Danny McGrory had by chance seen Bill the evening the gun arrived in Wiseton Road – and before someone had evidently returned to bury it. There was something just as deadly travelling with it – as Danny would tell me almost eight years later:

'Bill had asked me to go round to his house and then go out for a drink,' Danny told me. 'When I arrived, he looked terrified, hands shaking as though something dreadful had happened. He kept repeating: "I don't know what to do."

'Dragging me into the kitchen, Bill then indicated a large holdall on the table. I looked in. I had only ever seen a sight like that in TV dramas. But I knew straightaway what it was.

'Bag upon bag of white powder, each neatly tucked against the next for maximum capacity. I wouldn't have a clue how much this amount of cocaine was worth, but I am guessing hundreds of thousands. Worse was to follow as Bill lifted the bags and took out, to my absolute horror, a gun that was lying underneath.

'I said: "For God's sake, Bill, put it down. Your fingerprints will be all over it."

'We both looked at one another, not knowing how to behave

in the middle of a scene we had only ever encountered in fiction. I was suddenly very, very angry. I remember barking at him: "What do you think is going to happen if the glass in that window suddenly smashes and we find ourselves part of a police raid? What am I going to say as an explanation of why I am standing in front of half a tonne of cocaine and a revolver? That I just popped in for a drink? Don't drag me into all this, Bill. It's not fair." '

Danny said that Bill looked shell-shocked – and, nodding apologies to Danny, admitted he had been so shaken by being left with the bag that he had not taken in the implications of Danny's accidental involvement.

I myself did not then know about the vast amount of cocaine in Bill's house. But I knew about the alleged gun – and that was bad enough. Bill was in big trouble, of that I had no doubt.

'What's it all about, Bill, what have you done?' I would ask with overwhelming weariness shot through by gnawing anxiety. But all he ever talked about was Alex, bewildered and distraught – 'but I love her' being his sole response to any form of discussion or questioning. It was both the explanation for his behaviour and the shifting of blame.

Could I not see the poignancy of his tragedy? He could not bear her company, or rather the omnipresent cast of family and female friends she trailed in her wake, nor could he bear her absence. I wanted desperately to understand, to help him if I could.

But I could not stop him loving Alex. That was his decision.

14

About two months after my first meeting with gold-chained 'Barry' in the street outside Bill's house, I got a call from my brother, again sounding terribly distressed. Following yet another argument with Alex, he said he had been on his own at home when 'Barry' (his name, I would discover later, was Barry Fennell) had phoned saying he needed his help. Half an hour later Kevin's friend had arrived, handing him a carrier bag which he asked Bill to look after for him for a few hours.

Like a fool, Bill had agreed, without looking, or so he claimed, at the contents. After Barry had gone, Bill had opened the bag – to find himself staring at hundreds of thousands of pounds in cash. He said he did not have a clue where the money had come from or why it should need taking care of. He was, and not surprisingly in the circumstances, 'shit scared'.

Carrier bags containing thousands of pounds, people being beaten up with baseball bats, car-chases, a Smith and Wesson revolver buried in the garden, or so he said. Was it all fantasy? Bill had described Kevin and his friends as small-time crooks – not the Lavender Hill mob out of *Reservoir Dogs*.

I was too scared myself to do anything else but suggest he came round to me, minus the cash, as soon as he could. Minutes later, Bill rang again, saying that he could hardly leave that amount of money while he popped out for a coffee, so, on second thoughts, he had better stay put and wait for Barry to come back.

I kept him talking, convinced that if I badgered him long enough I could find out what was going on – to what extent he was involved with Barry and his bag of money.

But for once there was nothing doing. Making noises about how Barry might have 'won it on the horses' (even I wasn't naïve enough to believe this one), my brother was neither going to own up to any wrong-doing of his own or divulge any further information about anyone else's. He was also trying desperately, I felt, to distract me from anything he might inadvertently have revealed earlier.

I heard nothing from him for the rest of the day. In between Joseph's naps, I kept distractedly phoning his house. There was no reply. I also rang repeatedly the following day, a Sunday, but the telephone stayed unanswered. The next I heard from Bill was his habitual call on arrival at *The Times* just after nine o' clock on Monday morning. His voice sounded warm and relaxed, without the slightest trace of anxiety.

I asked, no doubt somewhat hysterically, what had happened after we had last talked. Bill, infuriatingly, dismissed the incident almost airily: 'Oh that . . . It was all right in the end. Barry came back in the evening and collected it.' He could have been talking about a neighbour's misdirected post. It was also clear from the way in which he spoke that he wanted no further questioning – particularly on an open line.

It was as if he had had some kind of warning. The confessions of what might be going on behind the drawn curtains at Wiseton Road stopped abruptly. Bill seemed less frightened, back in control. But I did notice that he was drinking, at first without apparent effect, far more wine when he came to visit us in the evening than he had ever done before.

Christy seemed able to put up with it, the maudlin outpour-ings in our kitchen, the expressions of impossible doomed love for Alex. I think my husband secretly enjoyed it, he and Bill were like adolescents again. One night I left them both downstairs until midnight with a bottle of vodka that Bill had brought round.

Early the next morning both of them were meant to go by train to a fishing port miles away in Cornwall for their different newspapers to report on some rebellion against the EU. Christy returned from the West Country the next evening with a tale of wandering round an empty fish-gutting hall looking for suitable interviewees with 'the worst hangover he had ever had'. When he had at last got there, the sought-after fishermen were all in the pub where Bill was buying them pints. My brother had got an earlier train and had filed his story within two hours of arriving. Bill still seemed indomitable, still capable of functioning when having drunk enough the night before to have felled an ox. But that, in a way, was no cause for comfort.

By the beginning of 1997, Bill was again talking about being short of cash. Selling the house in Wiseton Road and buying somewhere in Oxfordshire with Alex were back on the agenda. Our earlier spat over family money had meanwhile been honourably resolved: that spring he had finally paid me my share of our mother's legacy locked up in his house. But that should not have broken him financially by any means. I knew that Bill was earning a substantial salary as chief reporter on *The Times*. Where was it going?

That summer, he and Alex enjoyed a three-week holiday in the West Indies. There had also been various other trips too, to take Max for assessment to the Peto Institute in Hungary, and to Lourdes, to pray for healing.

Alex was high maintenance. As far as I knew, her only source of income was supplementary benefit plus a disability allowance for Max. Yet she shopped from Knightsbridge stores and did not have a job other than taking care of her son. Perhaps Bill was just finding it hard going having to subsidise his girlfriend's expensive habits?

Barbara Jones had been an independent and high-earning woman in her own right, and Ruth had always had at least a part-time job. Now, for the first time in his predominantly bachelor life, Bill was having to support two other people as well as himself. But it was not just money worries that were weighing him down, I knew that.

A 'gun in the garden' – bags of cash in the bedroom. He would not tell me anything more about that – and even if he had chosen to do so, I really, really did not want to know.

15

Bill's mask of control was beginning to break. The jokes were still coming, but fewer now and costing him greater effort. He also looked almost permanently exhausted, skin pale and eyes so starved of sleep that his expression was one of constant strain. The lack of money, and his latest bust-up with Alex, now seemed the only topics that animated him. He would go on and on about Alex for hours. My questions about money – where it was going – were met by cold anger.

By the end of March that year I was dimly aware he had twice remortgaged his house, on both occasions claiming he needed the extra cash to repay his debts. What these were, he would not tell me. A few weeks later he announced that even the last amount, £15,000, was not enough. He needed more.

What I did not know was that Bill had been gambling, both on horses and in casinos. His colleague Danny McGrory told me later of a conversation with Bill around this time: 'Bill told me one day he owed one bookie well over a thousand and yet was still placing bets, always in cash, of hundreds at a time.' Horses? Bookies? Bill had his vices, but gambling was never one of them. I had never known him to show the slightest interest in racing, which I remember him describing as 'a mug's game'. He could not even understand Christy's love of playing poker every few months in north London with his raffish-enough friends for small amounts of money, far less risking thousands.

Then suddenly he called me one morning sounding much more cheerful:

'It's all sorted,' he said. 'Kevin is going to lend me the money.'

Knowing what little I did of Kevin, I had heard enough of guns and baseball bats not to want my brother in his debt. Desperately I tried to talk Bill out of it.

'There must be another way. Why don't you go back to the bank again? Does Alex know about this?' Bill said she did not. Nor did he tell me straightaway about the loan's little catch.

I would hear about this a few weeks later. It had been agreed in April that Bill would repay Kevin's 'loan' by paying the rent for a 'caravan' at a place called Pagham on the Sussex coast. It was apparently to be a holiday home for Alex's and Kevin's mother, and somewhere too where Max could be looked after. The arrangement seemed benevolent enough.

In a bizarre twist, after mentioning to Bill that I needed more help in the house, Kevin's and Alex's mother, Bridget, offered to come and work as my occasional cleaner. As Bridget did not drive, I agreed to go and pick her up from her home in Fulham. Often we would chat in the car, or sometimes over a cup of tea in the kitchen after she had finished her work. One day she mentioned that her daughter-in-law, Lena, was going to take the children to the caravan at Pagham. Bill had told me Kevin was 'away on business', and expected to be gone for several weeks. I knew that Lena had recently given birth to a third child – this time a boy, named Harry. I said to Bridget that it seemed tough on Lena to be left on her own so much with three small children.

Although Bill and I still continued to speak at least once a day on the phone, he had little contact with Joseph who was always in bed and asleep by the time Bill called in the evenings. So I was surprised, as well as touched, when Bill suddenly offered one afternoon in late October 1997 to look after Joseph at our house while I drove up to visit our daughter Katy at the Royal Free Hospital in Hampstead where she was now a medical student.

Leaving Katy at about four o'clock that afternoon, I hit rush hour on the Edgware Road and was held up for nearly an hour. But I was not too worried. I still trusted Bill, knowing that although he could occasionally be careless or disorganised, I could always depend on him on the big things, like taking care of my baby.

It was getting on for six o'clock when I finally reached Wandsworth, happily imagining what Bill and Joseph would get up to in my absence – watching television or sitting on the floor playing with Duplo.

There were no lights on in our house. By now it was completely dark, and since our house is almost totally glass-fronted I could see straight into the downstairs room. There was no one there.

I tried to remain rational. Perhaps Bill had taken Joseph round the corner to his house. Or Alex had arrived and they had taken both children out somewhere? My heart was thudding hard. A voice inside my head reminded me – I had had my mobile phone on me all the time. Why hadn't Bill called and told me what they were doing?

Perhaps there had been an accident? Bill might have taken Joseph straight to Casualty – especially, and this thought caught at my throat, if it was urgent and he did not want to frighten me.

But I am frightened now, I thought. Where are they? I wanted my baby son now, this moment, safe, smiling, back in my arms. By this time my hands were shaking so much I could barely fit my key in the lock. Calling out for Bill repeatedly, I entered the cold, deserted hall. I ran from room to room downstairs – all empty. No lights, no television, not the slightest sign of anyone in the house at all. I ran up the first flight of stairs on to the landing and looked up. Our house is open plan so the upper floor was visible from here. Then I saw them.

Slumped flat-out on the sofa Bill lay snoring, Joseph spread-eagled on top of him face-down and still. Was he breathing? I shot up the remaining stairs and across the room so fast I stumbled, tripping over Bill's feet and almost falling on top of them. Joseph stirred, rolling off Bill's chest and starting to whimper. Snatching my baby tight against me, I prodded Bill hard with my foot. I could feel myself shaking again now – but this time with total fury.

In that moment I decided. Never, never again could I trust Joseph to Bill's care. I must have been crazy to think I could in the first place. Something had happened, was still happening, to my brother that was beyond any comprehension.

I did not know whether to shout at him or burst into tears; I felt like doing both. Bill woke up and, finding himself being shouted at, responded in kind with a torrent of foul abuse – his habitual reaction to being confronted by an accusing woman. There was a flickering glimpse of guilt in his expression. My haranguing went quiet.

Once we both started to calm down, Bill told me he had enjoyed what he described as 'a great time', taking Joseph to Pizza Express at the top of the road, where Joe had been overwhelmed by a monster chocolate bombe while Bill, no doubt, put away several bottles of wine.

My brother was clearly very drunk indeed. I raged with emotion – not just fury with Bill for being drunk in charge of my son, but from terror of the unknown. My brother had always been so gentle and attentive around children, as well as responsible. What malign force could rob a grown-up human being of even this instinct? Bill by now was clearly unable to look after anyone, least of all himself. Still snarling and aggressive, although knowing he was now cornered, he did at least listen when I explained to him how dangerous it was to leave a one-year-old child asleep at the top of two flights of stairs.

By the end of that awful day I had forgiven Bill, of course, as I always did. What I did not realise was just how chastened he himself had been by the incident. After his death I sat down on the stairs at home and cried when I found this account of 'how your drinking or drug habit has affected your family' recorded in his confessional:

'My sister, with whom I was always very close, suddenly refused to trust me with her baby son any more,' Bill wrote, 'saying my behaviour had become unpredictable and "mad". At first I was furious. Afterwards I cried for hours.'

16

Somehow Bill still managed to function at *The Times*. He covered the big stories of the time professionally and stylishly – the Labour campaign and election victory of May 1997 and the death of Diana, Princess of Wales, later that summer. But when a new Balkan war looked like breaking out in Kosovo, Bill apparently expressed the utmost reluctance to go. It was so unlike him, the old warhorse who would once have begged the foreign desk for a dangerous assignment whenever the emotional going got tough in London. But outside the office at least, 'Alex' was all he would talk about – Alex and the Hanleys.

It was as if, I began to consider later, he had found a substitute for war. What he had seen in Bosnia had convinced him perhaps that life was unredeemably horrible. But he still craved the excitement, the adrenaline, the risk-taking. Maybe the transitory glamour of Kevin Hanley with his alleged gun and his bags of money provided a substitute, right there in his own suburban kitchen. Alex came as part of the package after all.

Meanwhile, the more prosaic demands of the domestic news agenda had to be met if he were to keep his job. He was moved to features – writing longer, reflective pieces rather than following the news with the pack. Hunting on his own, the solidarity of the newsroom began to unravel.

It was a strange feeling reading his journalism on a computer screen in a gloomy newspaper library – hundreds of pieces going back to the early 1990s. I could picture Bill at his desk taking my calls as he bashed them out, telling me politely enough when he was on deadline that it was time to go. Then of course he would ring me back to seek my advice on some new Alex-based dilemma – his own dramas revolving round the work he was making for the day. What could I find in the words he had left behind?

That October he interviewed the late George Best, the alcoholic footballer, who was accompanied by his new wife, a twenty-two-year-old former air hostess, also called Alex. Bill's story ended with a quote. Reading it years later it might have been written in code: 'I know there are days when I'll want to go off on a jag, Alex knows that too,' said Best. 'There are dark moods and demons, you just have to go off and get wrecked. The difference is that now I can keep booze under control. I have Alex and a lot to look forward to . . .'

Bill, it struck me, might have been vocalising some inner wish of his own – the clandestine addict interviewing the very public one. His own behaviour around Alex Hanley had meanwhile become even more aggressive and argumentative if that were possible. She would simply refuse to see him when he was in one of these moods. That just made things worse.

Bill was also socialising less and less frequently with any of his colleagues. Danny McGrory recalled that Bill always: 'compartmentalised his life in this way, keeping the people who made up all the different parts completely separate from one another'. And Pat Bishop remembered: 'Whenever Bill and I did meet up, then it was always arranged as a boys' night out, just the two of us. If I even asked how Alex was, Bill would change the subject immediately, often behaving as if he was embarrassed by the relationship.' His Wapping colleague Richard Duce remembered: 'Alex came first – before everything.'

Alex's flaky world had become a different planet from which Bill might fitfully emerge to the realities of journalism – with its deadlines, responsibilities and wobbly enough certainties of continued salaried employment. Journalism's stimulations – of getting the story, of cracking the first paragraph, of creative writing, of boozy sessions with colleagues after the job was done – were clearly no longer enough. Alex's world was winning.

One evening in that autumn of 1997 I saw for myself. We were invited to a meal at a restaurant that one of Alex's friends had just opened on the Thames at Richmond. Alex had also invited, Bill said, about ten others, some of whom we had met before, some not. None of them were journalists or friends of Bill's.

I felt uneasy from the moment I sat down at the table. Although from a distance the other guests had appeared to be talking and laughing as anyone might, up close I felt a different current in the air. Again, as at the party at Wiseton Road eighteen months earlier, there was a Mad Hatter's air about the conversation, an unpredictable and hysterical feel to what was being said. A number of the guests laughed too loudly, or too long, performing dolphins standing on their tails, clapping their fins on command at jokes and anecdotes of crashing banality.

Bill was sitting near to me, and although at first very attentive, seemed to become progressively agitated as the crazy assembly rambled on. There was also an irritatingly frequent migration to the toilet, both by him and the other guests, heads bobbing up and down and people shoving past one another in constant procession.

Bill always said I was naïve. I had no desire to join the queue for the lavatory to go through the ritual of the razor blade and the rolled-up £20 note. But it was clear enough what was going on.

Conversations became unconnected, with no one paying the slightest attention to what the person sitting beside them had just said, non-sequiturs flying like bread rolls back and forth across the table, while some just sat chuckling hyena-like into their oversized plates.

Not surprisingly – given the unappetising nature of the 'fusion' bowl of thick, shiny black bean soup that now stared back at me, a white dollop of cream glistening queasily on its surface – there was not much interest in the food by our fellow diners either.

Meanwhile, Bill seemed to grow both more morose and more aggressive by the moment, bridling against being gently told off by Alex for his increasingly insulting remarks about her friends. At first she was teasing, but Bill leapt at the opportunity for confrontation. His language switched from mildly insulting to the outright abusive, alarming those, including Christy and me, who were still sufficiently aware to notice. He was really getting into it now.

Alex was fighting back, her female friends rallying behind her – Bill's still-just-about-literate rants providing the drama this drug-coarsened audience had clearly expected all along. But as I watched the two of them centre-stage, they were not Sid and Nancy. They were turning into Terry and June.

By eleven o'clock we had had more than enough, thankfully saying goodbye and gratefully stumbling back along the now pitch-black towpath to our car. Never have the words 'an evening from hell' seemed so appropriate a description.

Bill called early from the office next morning, telling me that he and Alex had had a blistering argument after leaving the restaurant. They were now, temporarily at least, estranged. Not much new there. He confessed to me that he had hated the whole outing and had never wanted to go in the first place. His behaviour had proved that at least. The whole thing had been braindead, shaming, abysmal.

'What's the matter, Bill?' I asked. 'I don't mean about last night, but generally?'

Bill answered hesitatingly: 'I don't know, I'm not sure, Clare . . . I guess I don't know who's in charge of the train any more.'

I sort of understood what my brother meant, and half recognised what he had said as a quote from a poem. Only since his death have I discovered the stanza in full:

> Who is in charge of the clattering train
> The axles creak and the couplings strain;
> And the pace is hot, and the points are near
> And sleep has deadened the driver's ear;
> And the signals flash through the night in vain
> For Death is in charge of the clattering train

Had I myself known that last apocalyptic line at the time, Bill's throwaway remark would have scared me witless. But my brother knew the line. I believe he knew who was in charge all along. It was just that when he admitted it, it was already too late.

In an entry in his confessional diary written three years later, Bill wrote: 'As my addictions gained strength the prospect of being without terrified me. I concealed cocaine wraps down the spines of books and vodka in the boot of the car. One spring evening, having finished the vodka, I pulled every book from the shelf searching for drugs. At last I found a packet just as my girlfriend came home. She left, in disgust, two minutes later . . .'

And in another he wrote: 'While staying with friends in Oxfordshire I got up during the night and crept downstairs to the living room where I knew my host had a big bag of cocaine. I spent the next hour using his drugs. I had never stolen before, but any remorse I felt was chilled out by the coke.'

17

In the spring of 1998 Bill announced he was going to sell his house. When I urged him not to, he refused to listen. The market was flat, but Bill did not seem to care. It was clear, however, that it had to be done as quickly as possible. He had remortgaged so many times, so I supposed, that the sale would not realise much cash anyway. Whatever might be left, he seemed to need it right now. It was sold to a speculator for a seemingly pathetic amount. His furniture, books, all the stuff from our childhood home that our mother had brought when she had moved in six years before, disappeared into some lock-up.

Where was he going to live? It seemed plain to Bill – Alex would have him to live with her in the country. Why shouldn't she? 'Fuck her nagging about drugs,' he would mutter in my hearing.

Who could blame her? In Bill's Priory confessional diary he dispassionately described the events of his birthday, 4 September 1998, spent in the country with Alex: 'Three grams of coke, two bottles of champagne and a dozen beers later, I woke up to find an empty dinner table,' he wrote. 'In front of me was an untouched lobster and an unopened present. My partner had prepared a birthday dinner and invited some friends. I had passed out early. I found her sobbing silently upstairs. "Please, please, stop," she said. "You're driving us apart and killing yourself." I recall simply shrugging before going to bed.'

Once again Alex showed him the door. He was now effectively homeless. Bill started the restless motorway pounding again, driving his powerful BMW into Wapping, back to the country to beg his girlfriend for forgiveness – or to anywhere a not over-judgmental female would have him.

Bill had by now re-established contact with Barbara Jones. She was naturally wary, but on his pitiful turnings-up on the doorstep of her Wiltshire cottage she seemed prepared to take him in. Barbara would tolerate his presence for a few days before Bill would smash it up all over again.

After that he would sofa-surf, staying with whoever would put a roof over his head for a night, until finally managing to persuade Alex to forgive him. But she would not, most certainly not, have him actually living with her. She fixed him up in some council-owned flat in Fulham, the top floor of a nineteenth-century terrace house, ostensibly tenanted by 'friends'. It was near her mother, Bridget. I never went there; I had no desire to. The arrangement did not last long. Even his dodgy landlords at last found his presence unacceptable. Alex's friends evicted him after a couple of months, and they rang me angrily to demand I come to take away his clothes and clear up the mess. I refused – Bridget and Alex at least did that.

These periods when Bill was between women were some of the most difficult times for me personally. He was welcome enough in our house for an early evening drink, but Christy looked ever more agitated if he showed any signs of intending to stay. He had made it very clear he did not want Bill using drugs anywhere near Joe. But now Christy began to actively dislike him visiting – even telephoning. He confessed later that he would leave a modem on all day to block the manic stream of telephone calls. Still he was his brother-in-law, one of his oldest friends. There had to be some chinks in my husband's armour. He would only have Bill in the house, he conceded, under controlled conditions – and certainly not staying overnight.

It was heartbreaking for me; Christy obviously now felt he must protect his family from his own friend and brother-in-law. It all seemed a long and tragic road from the days of their Oxford intimacy, the double act that Pat Bishop still remembered so fondly.

My own inner conflict was almost unbearable. My love for my

brother was now in direct opposition to my love for my husband and son. Apart from all this, Christy had his own preoccupations. He had resigned from his job at the *Sunday Telegraph* and now laboured all day at the India Office Library in Southwark or at the kitchen table, writing a very serious-sounding book about an Indian maharajah – even giving up drinking for a month to get on with it. Bill found his actions totally baffling.

My husband, himself always a heavy drinker, told me later about strange early evening sessions in the kitchen as I put Joe to bed, giving Bill old-fashioned temperance lectures on the joys of sobriety and the evils of drink, how it destroys not just love for others, but love for oneself. Bill's face would flicker like a wonky television picture, he said. The old deep intelligence was there for a second, then it would fade. They would talk, laugh, joke, then Bill would just stare out of the window, before Christy propelled him thankfully towards the front door and out into the street. I always thought Bill's own self-love would save him. Christy warned me it might not.

I was stuck. Bill's deepening despair was obvious – even if it was wrapped in fatuous tirades against Alex and her unwillingness, as he expressed it, 'to commit'. His intake of drink, and whatever else, was now off the dial. He was destroying himself in front of me.

Bill could not conceal the drinking, even if snorting cocaine remained a secret ritual – at least when I was around. 'Why, why do you drink so much?' I would plead. 'Why all that vodka?' Bill would not answer, but others on the fringes of his dwindling universe would tell me why. 'He needs it to come down from the coke,' offered someone or other by way of explanation – as if a litre of Stolichnaya in the morning was a simple hangover cure. 'Vodka and cocaine mix together in the body to make a new drug,' someone blandly explained.

As Bill increasingly became oblivious to his surroundings, stumbled over his words, seemed to forget whole chunks of his life or our childhood, there was terrifying talk of something called 'wet brain' – incipient drug- and alcoholic-induced dementia. When my brother's mind refused to shut down even for sleep, the answer was simple: Rohypnol, the heavy-duty tranquilliser. When I myself found sleep all but impossible with worry, someone even offered it to me, a small pill screwed into a tissue, pressed consolingly into my palm. I binned it immediately.

Cocaine culture, I was discovering, has its codes, rules and secret economy. It also has its own lawyers, accountants and physicians. At every turn some quack remedy seemed to be on offer, some half-baked description of what was going on in Bill's brain chemistry. He was awash with booze and depressants, not to keep him functioning in the real world, but to make him still capable of 'using'. He needed help, real help.

It sounded so clunky, so melodramatic, but that Bill needed urgent professional medical intervention could not have been clearer. Alex and I now talked urgently on the phone about what to do. I was happy enough to deal with her. She, after all, was still the object of Bill's obsession. She had stated her terms: Bill either got clean or she would leave him for good. If there were any sanction that might make Bill stop, surely that was it. It was down to me meanwhile to do something practical about it. Bill was not going to be a willing patient.

Ironically he himself had written a newspaper feature that summer about treatment for addiction – a profile of a 'celebrity asylum' then attracting media attention for its famous clients. Reading it years later – as with the interview with George Best – I found it full of clues and portents:

'Tranquil and secluded with attentive staff and gourmet food, the Priory Hospital, an exclusive clinic in southwest London, provides a safe haven for the rich and famous – at £330 a night,' Bill had written. One patient that he had interviewed, described as a 'successful restaurateur', told him: ' "Having binged on drink and drugs for 72 hours, I accused my wife of having an affair with a neighbour . . . We were having a barbecue and suddenly the craziness took over. I thought this guy was winking at my wife and became convinced the children were his, not mine."

'Pat Hall (not his real name) cannot remember the

rollercoaster ride of violence, remorse and physical collapse that saw him admitted to the Priory,' Bill's story continued. 'He was sobbing and gibbering all the way. But he had stashed cocaine in his shoe . . . when his drugs were gone, Pat had to confront himself and his shame: "Sitting in my room one evening and watching the setting sun touch the garden, I knew I wanted to live and be a person, not an addict," ' Pat Hall had told Bill.

It was a strange feeling reading Bill's words written two years before his own admission to the very same addiction hospital. Did my brother equate his own condition at the time with the man he was dispassionately interviewing – the psychotic jealousy, the bingeing, the possibility of redemption? Did his interviewee even exist or was he rather an amalgam of Bill himself with someone he met that day?

There was enough in the story to convince me in distant retrospect that my brother was sending some kind of signal about his own plight – and a glimmer of acceptance that he too might 'need help'.

In mid-September he went on an assignment for *The Times* to South Africa. He returned after ten days in the sun looking dreadful, his skin grey and lined under the tan, his eyes hooded with fatigue. I would find out exactly why much later. In that moment when I saw him it was clear to me that something had to be done – and now. The trouble was persuading him.

I saw how his mind was working. I knew he didn't have any intention of giving up on drink or drugs. But by now I was so frightened of losing Bill that I didn't care. I was willing to take whatever he would concede and would have dragged him bodily to the door of any treatment centre that was willing to have him.

Bill might have begun to realise that going through what he would have seen as the 'mummery' of therapy was becoming inevitable. But somewhere in the recesses of his mind he thought he would miraculously emerge the other side – able to knock back the odd glass of wine or snort the occasional line. Bill just didn't get it, didn't understand the meaning of being an addict.

Yet he was one – and perhaps had been in one form or another throughout his entire life.

It seemed ironic that during my own career as a journalist, I had often interviewed addicts of various persuasions, as well as their doctors. My address book read like a private health directory. On the advice of friends who had had experience of going through rehab themselves, in early November I approached Dr Robert LeFever at the Promis Recovery Centre just outside Canterbury.

Much to my relief, he agreed to take Bill as soon as we could physically get him there. In the meantime, with Alex's help, Bill approached his employers and, through them, BUPA, to authorise the financing of his stay at Promis. I don't know who he saw and what was said at *The Times*, all I know is that the funding seemed to come through both effortlessly and instantly. He was going into rehab.

Within forty-eight hours of my first call to Robert LeFever, Alex had coaxed Bill into her car and was heading down the M2. I was reassured to hear within hours from a friend at Promis, Patrick Williams, that Bill was not only settling in, but had already enjoyed a first lunch of guinea-fowl and game chips. Patrick had formerly been an employee of Conrad Black at the *Telegraph* as boardroom chef and had entertained myself and my husband at a Christmas-eve feast (when all the bosses were away) at Canary Wharf. His cooking was amazing. He was also a talented flautist, but was now working as the critically acclaimed chef at Promis. Christy, on hearing the description of Bill's menu, claimed to feel envious of his brother-in-law's pampered environment, joking that he wanted to check in immediately.

I was not surprised. Patrick's cooking at Promis had filled more column inches of Sunday supplements than LeFever's methods of treatment. Patrick also told me that as Bill had arrived ill-equipped for the coldness of the Kent countryside, he had lent him a pashmina to keep him warm while undergoing the group therapy sessions.

It all sounded so very cosy and people-like-us – rehab with script by Richard Curtis, *Four Weddings and a Coke Habit*, complete with happy ending. But it was not happy, beginning, middle, nor end. Bill rang me within a few days: 'It's dreadful, this place, I'm not staying. Six o'clock in the morning alarms and group brainwashing . . . LeFever's a megalomaniac. I'm leaving . . .'

Bill lasted eight days – before demanding that Alex send his clothes by taxi from London and checking out. Distraught by Bill's defection, I rang Promis and spoke to Robert LeFever's son, Robin, a psychologist and counsellor, as well as being a former addict himself.

I can still remember what Robin told me that morning: 'Bill will get worse, Clare. He's already lost his house. He'll spiral down further. Next he'll lose his job and his girlfriend. If that doesn't stop him . . .'

Robin didn't have to say any more, and I didn't want him to. Never having had to confront the possibility of Bill's death so starkly before, I told myself it wouldn't happen. I wouldn't let it. Robin was exaggerating, I reassured myself, perhaps in the hope of frightening Bill back. But Robin would be proved right, even down to the running order.

18

Bill returned promptly to the *The Times*, whose management seemed to have no qualms at all about his busting out of Promis. Having laboured so hard to get him into treatment in the first place, I was not quite so understanding. But Bill assured me that all he needed was to 'get back to the grindstone' in order to get sorted out. He was, however, now moved formally full time from the newsroom 'upstairs' to the features department, which apparently had a more structured routine. The move would prove to be catastrophic.

Danny McGrory remembered him powering through his features work in the morning, then, having filed a beautifully written piece, either hanging round the newsroom distracting colleagues who were still chasing stories or drinking the afternoon away alone in Wapping pubs. 'He just didn't seem to want to go home,' said Danny.

Bill himself recorded: 'Having swapped from being a war correspondent to a features writer, my drinking increased. I tried to get all my work done before 2.00 p.m. so I could prop up the bar all afternoon. It soon became obvious and the features editor told me that my behaviour had not gone unnoticed. I was furious – even though the warning was in my best interests.'

The South Africa assignment, a story about the children of Nelson Mandela which Bill wrote up just before the doomed admission to Promis, had been a disastrous precursor to the new regime. Work still came first – *just*. Then he would get out of it. His confessional diary written in the autumn of 2000 of his time in Johannesburg two years before revealed:

'The job done, I went on a drinking and cocaine sniffing spree before calling the office. As bad luck would have it, I got through to the features editor immediately. She knew I was off my head and said: "Please stop this, Bill. I am so worried for you. You're a talented journalist but you are destroying yourself." I put the phone down without a word.'

But Bill at least still seemed to be functioning: driving into Wapping from Alex's house in the country – or from whatever London sofa he had managed to find to sleep on the night before. Work was still the refuge.

Then something happened. At around nine o'clock one evening late that month, 28 November 1998, Bill arrived outside our house, banging so urgently on the door that I was really frightened. Christy wearily let him in. He stood in our little hall looking so utterly desperate that he scared me. Reaching up to kiss him as he came into the kitchen, I noticed how suddenly less substantial he seemed, his clothes loose and flapping around his body. His breath and his coat carried a distinct whiff of wine. There was something else that Christy noticed – a smell of old fireplace about him, a bit like burned vegetation.

Bill shuffled crab-like sideways across the room, crumpled into the nearest chair, put his hand up to his forehead and blurted: 'Kevin's been arrested by the police.' Alex had apparently told him, I would later learn, by phone an hour or so before.

Bill was behaving like a madman, his eyes blazing, his head jerking at the slightest distraction. 'What is it?' I pleaded with him, 'why are you behaving like this?'

'You don't want to know,' he replied. 'You don't want to go there.' His nose was running like a tap.

Every now and again he would take a deep long snort, blocking off one nostril as if trying to clear his nasal passages. Christy looked as if he would like to hit him.

'He's not staying here,' Christy barked. He seemed set to frogmarch him out of the house. Bill, crazily, had driven to our house in the BMW.

'You can't let him drive,' I pleaded. 'He'll kill himself or someone else.'

Bill looked like a wounded animal, eyes rolling, wracked with anguish. He stared at me – begging for some kind of release from the pain. Christy would not be moved.

'I can see when I'm not fucking welcome,' Bill grunted.

'Just get him out of here,' Christy sighed. Somehow we got him into a minicab. In a fit of credit-card-waving bravado, Bill announced his intention of staying at the Conrad Hotel in Chelsea Harbour. God knows why there. I would find out later.

Kevin's arrest, temporarily at least, seemed to unite Bill and Alex in a common purpose. For a while he calmed down, appeared more sober, chastened even. His clothes were smart again. The events in our kitchen that November night were erased from his memory. I would discover that fact much later when I read in his Priory confessional: 'I woke up in the Conrad Hotel one morning without a clue as to how I got there.'

In the weeks that followed Bill would tell me about some of it – speaking in a strange new vocabulary, half criminal slang, half legalese, Kevin's 'brief', 'conspiracy to supply', 'copping a plea'. But what Kevin Hanley had actually done, who Kevin Hanley really *was*, he would not reveal.

This is what I could make out: Alex's brother had for some reason been stopped in his car in which cocaine had been found, though just how much Bill would not say. All I could get out of him was that Bill was urging Hanley to plead guilty. Kevin's solicitor apparently thought the opposite – and so did Alex. It was a big issue between them. Their common front rapidly dissolved. The rows were soon back and worse than ever.

Bill's solution to the crisis was predictable. He got out of it. He'd sit in our kitchen on increasingly sporadic evening visits glugging back wine, moaning about his inconsiderate girlfriend and saying as little as possible, even when rolling drunk, about what was really going on. There were a number of trips by Bill and Alex to see Kevin who was on remand in Wandsworth Prison, that much I knew. Bill confided to me that he 'bloody hated' these visits, and deliberately 'tanked himself up' to survive the ordeal.

'Why do you go, Bill . . . what hold's he got over you?' I would ask.

My brother would not reply – he just got more drunk. Alex, predictably, showed him the door.

Bill's solution to this new crisis was also predictable – he went back to Barbara Jones.

To my astonishment, the two of them arrived unannounced to see us one evening. It was now coming up to Christmas, and this being Barbara's first introduction to our now two-year-old son Joseph, it seemed an opportunity for a celebration.

Bill had, on Barbara's advice, visited Hamley's toyshop in Regent Street, and bought Joseph a traditional wooden farm set. Sitting down cross-legged on the floor in front of his round-eyed nephew, he opened the parcel and laid it out for him. It would have been the perfect happy family scene, had Bill not seemed so frighteningly disoriented, laughing manically at Joseph as the two of them played together.

Barbara immediately began a discussion about Kevin's arrest in an urgent, fact-finding way, while I kept a nervous eye on Bill as he bent down over my son. Unfortunately, Joseph, who must have been going down with an end-of-term nursery bug, chose that particular moment to empty the contents of his stomach into Bill's lap.

It was funny really. Bill thought it was anyway. The farcical element continued when Bill lay sprawled on the sofa in borrowed trousers listening to loud rock music through head-phones like some dysfunctional teenager. 'Look at him,' said Barbara, 'he's never grown up.' Her presence was somehow reassuring. Flaky Alex was in no position to 'save' my brother. Barbara Jones was bossy certainly, but if Bill needed someone forceful to propel him back to reality – it was now. Barbara meanwhile was working on a plan of her own.

A new year was coming. Bill wrote an events-of-1998 round-up for *The Times* features pages. It was frothy and cynical, a survey of celebrity pratfalls and royal embarrassments, but still funny. It contained this curious entry: 'The Priory, an exclusive clinic in southwest London, has never done so well, in terms of publicity at least . . . 1998 has been the year to get elegantly wasted and cured . . . if you can afford £3,000 a week.' Bill's own wasting had been anything but elegant. Nor had he been cured.

In the first few months of 1999 I now had reason to worry about another adult in the family as well as Bill. Our cousin Martin, the only son of our mother's twin sister, was then living in Bristol, having left his job as a bank official to take care of his elderly father. Our uncle had died, and Martin was now living a lonely existence in a neatly ordered house in a suburb of Bristol. Neither Bill nor I had ever been close to Martin, a kind, devout but somewhat sad bachelor now in his early fifties. He seemed to have been a permanent fixture since my earliest childhood.

Then one day Martin rang to tell me that he had been diagnosed with cancer. I promised we would come and see him as soon as we could. We would all go – including Joe, who Martin seemed to have a special affection for. I was glad to get the chance to talk – to feel that I had an older male relative I could rely on. In our conversation I found myself confiding what was happening to Bill – his out-of-control drinking, his deepening distress. In spite of his own anguish, Martin instantly began to look for a way in which he could help.

Arriving at my cousin's house the following weekend, I was shocked at how ill he looked. But it was good to see him, and over lunch at a local pub he visibly started to relax and enjoy himself. Towards the end of the meal, Christy took Joseph off to play outside to give us an opportunity to talk alone.

Martin leant forward across the table conspiratorially and said: 'Clare, there's something I want you to know. I've changed my will. Not that I'm planning to die just yet of course. Before all this, I was going to leave my estate to you and Bill. But now, and especially since Joseph was born, I've decided to leave money to the girls and Joseph instead of to you two direct. If Bill has any children before I die, or has any I don't know of, a share will go to that child as well.'

I did not know what to say other than to thank him. I did not want him to die, of course, and from the optimistic prognosis he assured me he had been given, it did not seem to be something that would happen for many years. I did not mind whether Martin left his money to me or to my children – I had not been expecting him to leave me anything in the first place.

I felt it better not to tell my brother of Martin's intentions – that was down to him. Bill would find out, eventually. He would not be happy.

19

Robin LeFever, the director of Promis, had spelled out the timetable of an addict's fall – loss of house, loss of job, loss of relationship. The first had long since happened, now the endgame at *The Times* was coming. Even his prodigious talent could not save Bill from professional disaster. An account from his own confessional diary recorded his behaviour in those weeks following Kevin Hanley's arrest:

'I was sent to Belfast to interview a recovering gambling addict,' Bill wrote. 'After drinking both before the flight at Heathrow and also onboard the plane, I was extremely drunk by the time I arrived. Yet instead of using a taxi, I still drove a hire car from the airport to interview the man at his home.

'When I returned to London, I couldn't even read my shorthand notes. I had to call the man and redo the interview over the telephone. It was totally humiliating as it had been obvious to him at the time how drunk I had been. At the end of our call he observed: "You've got a problem, mate." I was devastated.'

By now he was not even trying to hide his cravings from his colleagues. Pat Bishop remembers attending a dinner party with Bill in early 1999 hosted by the veteran foreign correspondent Dessa Trevisan at her flat in Albany. The evening was a reunion for war correspondents who had reported from Bosnia:

'Everyone had had a lot to drink by the time the party broke up just after midnight. But Bill was desperate for the evening to continue and suggested going to a club afterwards.

'I was tired and told him I'd rather go home to bed. I

remember Bill turned to me and said, "Are you sure? I know where we could get some crack if you want to try?" I looked back at him in amazement, wondering for a moment if he really meant it.

'I left shortly afterwards, but bumped into Bill the following morning in the Brompton Road. He looked very tired and dishevelled and when I asked him where he had spent the night, he told me he had slept in the car.

'I knew he had argued with Alex, but had not realised he had had nowhere to sleep. I asked him why he hadn't asked to stay at my flat and told him he was welcome any time he wanted. Then I suddenly understood – Bill had been too proud to ask.'

Events at Wapping were to become even grislier. Danny McGrory remembered Bill telling him sometime in early 1999 that he had just been caught 'free-basing' heroin in the office kitchen by a female colleague. Had she told anyone, reported it to management? Apparently not. Perhaps Bill had charmed her, he was always good at that.

Danny was horrified, not just by what his friend was doing in the first place and the casualness of where he chose to do it, but by his naughty schoolboy delight at getting away with it. 'Bill told me this appalling story with an edge of bravado in his voice,' so Danny would tell me. 'He just seemed to dismiss the crazy risk he was taking as if it were nothing at all.'

I could not know at the time, nor could any of Bill's friends and colleagues, that in those first weeks of the new year, the risk of getting caught taking drugs in the office was nothing to what was going on in the outside world. The parallel universe that Bill had for so long inhabited was falling to bits.

Early on the morning of Friday 12 February 1999 a huge police and Customs operation was mounted across southern England with a wave of dawn raids. Kevin's wife was one of the targets – Lena was arrested at the family house at 18 Bishops Road and taken, I would discover later, to Holloway prison. After a cryptic mention in a BBC Essex local radio bulletin, Customs got a judicial gagging order on any further press mention of the operation. There was nothing to say what was going on. Alex said nothing and neither did Bill.

Then on 1 March 1999 the *Racing Post*, not a journal I routinely read, published this story: 'An international arrest warrant has been issued for Brian Wright, a wealthy racegoer and gambler, following one of the largest-ever seizures of cocaine in Britain. Wright's son, also named Brian, is already in custody.

'Recently, Wright snr, a 52-year-old millionaire, is said to have been recovering from a heart-bypass operation at his villa in Spain. His current whereabouts are not known.

'The arrest warrant was issued on Wednesday. Twelve days earlier, on 12 February, Customs officers seized 440 kg of cocaine from a garage at Leigh-on-Sea, on the Essex coast . . .

'More than 150 officers were involved in the operation, which led to 13 arrests in eight different locations in the South East of England. Further arrests are expected . . .'

I did not see the story at the time. If I had, it would have been meaningless anyway. No other paper seems to have carried it, and nowhere were Kevin and Lena Hanley mentioned. But Bill must have read the story in the *Ra~ ~~ Post*, almost certainly. He was, as Danny McGrory told me yea   ~bling man after all.

My brother was by now h   Alex and
I found ourselves in that
Eastwick, incongruously u
Bill. Whatever dislike Bar
versa, a temporary truce

We were all agreed t
and quickly. We did n
wanted Bill to stay on
and use company hea
Not Promis this tim
LeFever, but the Pric
which Alex had hea

Barbara's plan, i
with his employers
called the 'Sierra

Barbara had heard about Sierra Tucson from a City trader friend who had successfully recovered there. It involved horse riding as part of the programme.

I myself was wary. I was deeply suspicious of anywhere whose promotional brochure stated: 'Love is like seeing the beauty of a sunrise behind the mountains, so pure and brilliant that our eyes fill with tears'. Bill would not have gone for that. I was also wary of the Arizona option because I knew that Bill needed a job to come home to – as and when he sobered up.

Of course he would. Of course he would get clean, I told myself. Of course Bill had a future – it was just a question of finding the right treatment.

Bill himself could not decide. One day he would be agreeing with Alex and me about staying on at *The Times*, the next threatening to resign immediately. He was too drunk to know what he was doing. In the meantime Barbara Jones was already talking to the counsellors at Sierra Tucson and was looking at provisional flight dates. Her will prevailed. One afternoon I took a call on my mobile from a desperate Alex telling me that Bill had decided definitely to quit his job, and could I try one last chance at talking him out of it? I called Bill straightaway. It was too late. Details of his severance pay had already been agreed.

20

Less than twenty-four hours after his departure to America on 29 March 1999, I received a late-night transatlantic telephone call. It was Bill: 'My God, Clare. What have I done?' he said. 'Have I really resigned? Do you think they might take me back?'

He then told me how, after waking up in his room in Sierra Tucson, he had for the first time in weeks experienced a sudden moment of clarity.

'I realise I have been off my head for days,' he said. 'I didn't know what I was doing at all . . . I just felt so desperate to be free of these compulsions. But I never meant to leave my job. Not ever . . .' But the deed was done. All I could do was give a sister's soothing advice. The first thing he had to do was get well, and all the rest would follow.

And so it seemed to go. I received late-night calls in which he progressively sounded fitter, saner, funnier. 'You'll never guess who I'm sharing a room with,' he would tell me. It was a famous rock star. 'Guess who's over the corridor . . .' It was a hugely famous Hollywood actress. The regime of horse-rides in the desert, good food, and an apparently less messianic approach to addiction therapy than he had encountered at Promis, seemed to be working. Best of all he was making plans for the future. Bill told me he had sent a fax to *The Times*, acknowledging his resignation but seeking reassurance he might be allowed to return as a contract writer following treatment. Their reply was guarded but held out some hope.

This time Bill did not bust out. He stayed the course – three months. He was coming home fit, clean and sober.

We arranged to meet for lunch at the Oriel restaurant in Sloane Square, the first day after his arrival back in London in late June 1999.

Bill looked wonderful, tall, tanned and once again filling his six foot two frame, loping towards me along the street, Alex tottering along in Jimmy Choo high-heeled ankle boots at his side. I threw myself into his arms, feeling his old bear-like hug, as strong and reassuring as it had been before.

We went inside and ordered lunch. Bill ordered a glass of red wine with his steak frites. I glanced across the table at Alex, who looked nervously back at me. Bill intercepted the look between us and laughed:

'Stop worrying all the time, the pair of you . . . Sierra Tucson is not like Promis . . . it's not about never being able to have a drink again.'

My own intelligence told me otherwise, but I wanted to believe him. True to his word, Bill stuck at two glasses, and was full of good humour. The only real moment of tension arose when he talked of finding somewhere to live. Alex said she was going to help him in flat-hunting, but he should not expect her to move in immediately.

Bill's expression flickered angrily for a second. Didn't she believe things would be different now? But he managed to remain, at least superficially, calm and rational. When we turned to the subject of his future, he appeared to have it all planned out. He talked of applying for jobs, freelancing at *The Times* and at other papers, as well as perhaps returning on staff.

'But, first,' he announced, 'I need to recover from the stress I have been through, have a few weeks relaxing in the garden.' He meant of course with Alex, who had moved houses while he had been away to yet another small village in Gloucestershire, and as always based herself near to several of her female friends. 'I intend getting myself completely better before going back to work,' Bill said. His plan sounded perfectly reasonable to me. In fact, it turned out to be a disaster.

Two weeks later Alex called me. Bill was drinking. He was not making the slightest effort to find work. The weather was hot and left Bill feeling indisposed to the idea of returning to a stuffy office. He was being manipulative, citing his addictive tendencies as a reason for not applying for jobs – the stress, he said, would bring the cravings back again.

He seemed to be living the life of some ageing rock star: boozing, loafing, arguing with Alex over some imagined slight. The whole thing seemed buoyed up by some expectation of easy money. Except there was no money. There was one trip to London that summer, but not, as far as I could make out, anything to do with finding a job. Bill would not see me or tell me why. I discovered the real reason much later. It was to stand bail for an alleged cocaine-supplier.

I would call him in the country – encouraging, coaxing, threatening him into being more positive. When he was in a good mood, he would agree, promising definitely to do something about sorting his life out, but always 'tomorrow'. On a bad day we would argue, Bill wondering why all the women in his life 'always had to be nagging at him . . .'

Alex's calls to me got more frequent. Arizona had not worked, she made it clear. Bill was more or less permanently drunk. He was also doing cocaine – lots of it. Where, I might have reasonably asked, was he getting it from in rural Gloucestershire, but I was too worried to make sense of anything. Then it got worse. Alex rang to say she could no longer have him around, Max was there at weekends, you know what that's like.

Bill, so Alex insisted, would have to find somewhere else to live – in London. At the time I felt Alex was being too harsh. Having read Bill's account of his own behaviour at this time, I can see her point: 'My partner has a very seriously disabled son and I had given her all the support I could until cocaine and alcohol sapped all my humanity and kindness this year – my rock bottom. I watched as she struggled to carry him, feed him or change his nappy. In the past I would have helped. One night I looked up from my reverie to see her staring at me with an expression of great sadness and incomprehension. I didn't care.'

Alex began urgently asking round her female friends as to whether any of them knew of somewhere Bill could stay. Towards the end of that summer of 1999 Alex heard from one of them, a woman called Claudia, who had a flat to let in Oxford Road, Notting Hill.

Alex now moved a virtually comatose Bill up to London. Bill was angry, of course, but by now even he recognised that his behaviour had become intolerable. He seemed to take the latest upheaval willingly enough. He was too out of it to care.

Then one morning I had an unexpected call from Barbara Jones. Bill had rung her to tell her he had moved. He had sounded very strange and a highly alarmed Barbara had driven to see him. She told me she had called on Bill at the Notting Hill address and discovered him in an almost catatonic state, fully dressed and lying on the bed, but unresponsive and very, very thin. She said that it took her such a long time to get him to speak and open his eyes that for a moment she had feared he was dead.

Terrified, I told her that Christy and I would get there straightaway.

Arriving at the flat, Christy was still parking the car while I approached the large Victorian house, which stood in dark-green shadow, overhung by trees and shrubs. My feet crunched on the gravel as I reached the steps and I thought I saw movement at a basement window. But when I pressed the bell, no one came to answer the door. I tried again, ringing . . . ringing . . .

By now Christy had joined me, and we began knocking and banging at the window, calling Bill's name. Just about to give up, I heard shuffling from the other side of the door, followed by the sound of several locks and bolts being released.

The door opened and a figure I barely recognised as my own brother stood there in front of me, swaying slightly, as old people might do after climbing steps. He looked seventy years old.

It was Bill all right, but Bill as I had never seen him looking in my life before. In the space of only a week or so, he had aged twenty years. Skeletally thin, his appearance was made more pitiful by the yellowing-purple of bruises round one eye. Someone had obviously punched him, hard, and as if this were not alarming enough, he seemed unable to breathe or walk normally, veering lopsidedly against the door-jamb as if almost on the verge of collapse.

'Bill . . .' I broke off, and suddenly, uncontrollably, started to weep.

'Hello . . . what's the matter?' he said. 'Why are you crying?'

'It's you, Bill,' I stammered brokenly, 'What's happened to you?'

Christy placed a supportive arm around me as we followed a half-limping, half-shambling Bill into the flat. It was a standard conversion, 1980s financial trader in taste, decorated with heavy cream Viennese blinds at the bedroom window and dark raspberry carpets. Not that Bill was at that moment in any fit state to know or care about his surroundings.

He sat down, alternately staring into space and making strange jerking movements. When the telephone started to ring persistently, he at first ignored it. I pointed out that it might be 'Alex trying to get through', but he simply reached over and, with a practised gesture, yanked the connection out of the wall.

I noticed he was shaking, at first only slightly, but, as I watched, more and more violently until his whole body appeared wracked with convulsions.

One word came into my head as I watched him: 'withdrawal'. But from what? Was it cocaine, was it heroin, was it crack? The word filled my mind with a dozen visions of hell – hooded figures, left lying broken and scarred, half-alive in their own detritus down dark alleyways.

I was terrified of him and for him. It was clear that Bill wanted us to go, either because he did not want us to witness some horrible ritual of addiction, or because he was feeling so ill.

After a few more words of empty reassurance from Bill, that he was 'fine, really' and I 'wasn't to worry', Christy and I left him to it. Outside I sat in the car for a moment before suddenly turning to my husband and blurting: 'He's going to die.'

I dropped Christy off at Notting Hill tube station. For the next half hour, I sat alone in the car, my head on the steering wheel, the tears again running unchecked down my cheeks. What could

I do? He looked as if he should be on a life support machine. Take him home? It was Bill's decision. He wanted to stay where he was – to be out of it.

It was only a matter of days before Alex and I were both receiving calls from Claudia. The neighbours were objecting to his presence, and anyway Bill himself was clearly ill and should be in a hospital.

That was, of course, true, but how were we to manage an admission to another hospital, and under what circumstances? The days of fancy rehab, of guinea-fowl suppers and riding horses across the sands of Arizona, were over. He had resigned his job. His former employers had no residual duty of care. He had no apparent money left.

Bill clung on grimly in that Notting Hill basement twilight for another seven days, doing and feeling God knows what. I had no desire and no energy left to find out. A week later Alex went to visit Bill, and while the two were out of the flat on some shopping trip, Claudia slipped in and locked the door from the inside. Alex was furious, but could get nowhere in further discussions with her erstwhile friend, who would agree only to return what few clothes and possessions Bill had left.

Alex would not take him back. Christy would not have him in the house. Desperate for somewhere and someone who would tolerate his by now impossible presence, Bill himself found the answer. Barbara Jones took him in.

21

One evening that September I got a call from our cousin Martin in Bristol. He had been admitted to hospital with breathing problems, but it wasn't anything to worry about – he expected to be discharged soon. We chatted for about half an hour.

He asked about Bill, about Joseph and the girls and seemed reluctant to talk about his own condition other than to reassure me. The following morning I was out shopping when my mobile rang.

'It's Bristol General Hospital here . . . I'm so sorry to have to tell you, but your cousin Martin is not expected to live . . . His consultant thinks it unlikely he will survive the next twenty-four hours. Is there anyone who could get here to be with him?' Perhaps Bill could get there quicker. I knew he was with Barbara in Wiltshire. I called him; he was as shocked and saddened as I was. He spoke to Barbara and was back on the phone immediately. 'Yes' – they would leave straightaway. By the time I got home, the hospital had called again. Martin was dead.

A week later I was standing at Bill's side at our cousin's funeral. Barbara had bought him in her car from Wiltshire. At a local hotel afterwards, in between making small talk with Martin's former bank colleagues, I tried to catch Bill alone. He was not drinking, but seemed under dreadful strain. His face was grim, his expression preoccupied, and he would say very little. He suddenly left less than an hour after the funeral, insisting he had to be somewhere urgently.

About a month later I received a letter from our cousin's

solicitors in Bristol. Bill had received the same letter and was on the phone to me within minutes. Martin's will granted a quarter share of his estate to my children, Maria, Katy and Joseph, to be divided equally with 'any children of William Robert Frost who reach the age of eighteen years'.

Bill was furious. Having read the will in far more detail than I had had the chance to do, it seemed that our cousin, after inheriting his parents' house in Wandsworth, had been a millionaire. Yet before he died Martin had decided to give three-quarters away to Catholic charities. What remained was, it seemed, to be inherited neither by myself nor Bill but by our children. Bill had no children. He swore, he ranted about Martin. He needed money, lots of money right now. His anger was next turned on me.

Worse, much worse was to come when both Alex and Barbara seemed to agree about something for once – that my daughters should donate some of their inheritance to Bill, as if he were some kind of worthy cause.

Christy was having none of it. Nor was I. Katy and Maria were at university and needed the money. What the girls did with their inheritance was their own business. I resisted all pressure to lean on the girls – both then, and as that pressure mounted in the months to come.

Bill's temper did not lessen. His behaviour round Barbara was now as abusive as it had been around Alex. Over the years Barbara had seen Bill drunk, she had tolerated him being rude to her friends. But this was different. He was hiding vodka bottles and cocaine wraps around her house – he was too out of it even to argue with her any more. No one could have put up with it. Lovers, ex-girlfriends and former colleagues could banish him from their beds or shoo him from their rumpled sofas. But I could not exclude him. I was his sister, connected by blood and an unconditional love.

A new test of that love was coming. I got a call from an exhausted Barbara Jones one evening telling me she was bringing Bill up to London from Wiltshire the following day and she would either drop him off with me or 'dump him on the pavement'.

I had to do something. Christy had now installed extra bolts and locks, physically and metaphorically. It was quite clear that Bill couldn't stay with us. I meanwhile would have to find somewhere he might at least be safe until I was able to find some new lifeline.

I thought of Dick Hearn, Bill's oldest schoolfriend. Bill and Dick had known one another since the age of two and been friends ever since. I too had known Dick all my life, later becoming very close to his wife, Bev, who, having spent many years lecturing in film studies, had become a freelance journalist. I knew, without having to ask, that they would both be willing to help. It would last twenty-four hours.

Although I had told Bev at length about Bill's worsening condition, neither she nor Dick had seen Bill for some time. Having moved from London after passing the Brixton family garage business into the hands of his nephew, Matthew, Dick had now retired in some style to a beautiful cottage in a small village near Exeter.

After talking to Barbara again later that day, we agreed that she would ring Dick herself. The next I heard was a call from Bev to confirm that Bill and Barbara were now speeding towards Devon in Barbara's smart Saab convertible. Years later, Bev told me about Bill's visit. She had not said a word at the time. Her account was movingly honest:

'Dick arranged to meet Bill and Barbara at the Mare and Foal in Yeoford . . . not far from us. Dick thought Barbara would stay for a quick drink, but instead she simply opened the door and let Bill out.

'Bill told Dick afterwards the two of them had had a furious argument on their way to Devon about Barbara's car. Apparently Bill had damaged the sunroof while loading her "keep-fit" equipment in the back seat, and she was now demanding Bill pay for the repair – while he was just swearing profusely.

'Dick and Bill then spent a few hours in the pub before coming back. I had been working in my office upstairs, but remember the shock I got when I saw Bill standing in the doorway. He was emaciated and unwashed, while his clothes looked as if he had borrowed them from someone else. Bill had always been such a snappy dresser. Now he was wearing an old pair of faded jeans, down-at-heel cowboy boots, and a beaten-up tweed coat pulled round his middle, accentuating his thin frame. He looked like a tramp.'

I myself knew those clothes well. They had become a kind of uniform.

'We sat down together, but it was impossible to have a conversation,' Bev continued. 'He was wired, like something out of a film, but was not acting. Each time the clock in our hall struck the quarter-hour Bill leapt out of his seat, shrinking against the wall and whispering "what the fuck is that?" – having no recollection we had already told him it was the clock several times already.

'He drank solidly for the rest of the afternoon, beer, until we went down to the pub again in the evening, where Bill insisted on buying us a meal. But he barely touched his food, instead tanking himself up on vodka.

'By the time we got home he was so drunk I was terrified he might fall asleep with a cigarette in his hand. We live in a thatched cottage, the place would have gone up in minutes. I took his packet of Marlboro and hid them in the washing machine.'

The next morning was just as bad, so Bev told me, and when Bill asked for a beer for breakfast Dick replied brusquely: 'You are not having a drink in this house at ten-thirty in the morning.'

'Bill accepted the rebuke without any of his usual backchat,' Bev recalled. 'But I had had more than enough. I whispered to Dick, "Please, just get him out of here".'

But even as Dick drove Bill to Exeter to put him on a train there sparked a sudden flash of the old intimacy between them. 'Dick told me he sorted out which platform Bill needed for the London train and made sure he knew exactly where he was going,' Bev told me. Bill had suddenly put his arms round Dick and the two embraced before a final 'See you, mate'. It was the last time Dick was to see his friend alive.

Bill was rumbling back to London, the parcel passed yet again.

Other than whimper sleeplessly into my pillow, I did not have a clue what to do.

22

There was someone who might help. I remembered Nick Charles, a former alcoholic I had interviewed for the *Mail* about a year earlier. He had made a remarkable recovery himself and, having won the respect of medical professionals, had subsequently won NHS funding to set up a clinic of his own. Known as the Chaucer Clinic on the site of the old St Bernard's Hospital in Ealing, west London, it was now the largest of its kind in the country.

From our interview, I remembered Nick as a kind and humane man as well as a very humorous one. At least I thought there could be no harm in talking to him. I phoned him to tell him about Bill. Nick needed no explanations. He had been there himself. Although he could promise no instant remedies, he immediately offered to help.

An appointment was made for Bill the following day – 7 February 2000 – for an 'initial assessment'. Christy offered to get him there. Now all I had to do was persuade Bill to go.

For once I did not need to try too hard. Bill had arrived back in London with, for the first time in his life, no job, no girlfriend and now not even a roof over his head. The dawn of the new millennium had come and gone – and I didn't even know where Bill was that night. Somehow he had survived the first weeks of the new year, sleeping in his car, in Holiday Inns, shuffling round the streets of Fulham still moping round Alex.

If the clinic agreed, if a bed was available and NHS funding could be found, he would then be admitted in the space of the next few weeks. Meanwhile I was desperate for some form of holding operation. Christy would not bend, but at least agreed that Bill would stay with us the night before the assessment. But where could he stay until his hoped-for admission?

I thought of our cousin, Sheilagh, formerly my father's partner in his practice in Kennington, and now a retired GP living alone in Sussex. Perhaps she would have him? Bill was compliant, grateful – and, on that wintry evening spent with us, for once he did not demand drink.

I put him in our daughter Katy's now empty room. He seemed to go off to sleep soundly enough. But an hour or two later he suddenly staggered into our bedroom – waking Christy with a start and terrifying me.

Bill's eyes were wide open. He was talking too, the words unclear and not addressed to either of us. Bill was sleepwalking, a habit I recalled from our childhood, one that always afflicted him when either deeply anxious or feeling guilty.

Christy and I lay awake the rest of the night. The next morning Bill disappeared into our bathroom for over an hour. There was no sound of water running, or of him doing anything at all. Christy was getting more and more agitated.

Eventually Bill came downstairs, white-faced and unsteady on his feet. I asked him what was wrong. He looked very scared. Then he said, 'I do really need help, don't I?' I didn't ask him any more questions. There was no need. Instead I put my arms round him. 'Yes, Bill. You do.'

Christy drove off with a trembling-handed but chastened Bill to attend his first assessment at the Chaucer. As soon as they had left the house I rang my cousin Sheilagh in Sussex. Trying to explain why I so needed her help was humiliating but essential.

To my overwhelming relief, Sheilagh agreed that Bill could come and stay with her while waiting admission if, that is, the Chaucer Clinic agreed to take him. Calling Christy on his mobile, I asked him to put Bill straight on a train to Sussex after the assessment.

On their way to Ealing, Bill and Christy stopped off at Bridget Hanley's house in Fulham, where the remainder of Bill's clothes had ended up. Bridget seemed frightened, refusing to open the door to him, so Christy would tell me afterwards. I was not surprised, Bill was frightening, but I could still feel angry.

Christy told me that evening about the long drive to the Chaucer. Bill was joking, telling him about wild times in celebrity-rehab in Arizona. They arrived at the former Victorian mental hospital; some sort of alcohol unit was signposted at the gate. 'Sorry, we're NHS,' a stern woman had told my husband as the two of them blundered about. 'And you need a doctor's referral – you want the charity bit in the stables round the back.'

Bill apparently had gone in passively enough. Christy meanwhile explored the derelict Gothic wards outside. The assessment over, he had driven Bill straight to Waterloo to get the train for the country. Bill had whistled an old soldiers' song – 'take me to the station . . . put me on the train' – half in resentment, half in humour, before waving goodbye like some wartime evacuee.

Calling my brother at our cousin Sheilagh's house that evening, he sounded maddeningly 'normal', happy and grateful to be settled somewhere at last. Forty-eight hours later I received a call from Nick Charles. Yes, the Chaucer would take Bill in about two weeks' time as and when a bed became available. I still remember his words: 'I can't make promises. Most of it is down to Bill. But I will do what I can to help save your brother's life . . .'

A health professional indicating that Bill's life hung by a thread was no longer a shock. Perhaps it really would all be OK now, I thought. Perhaps Bill would recover. Just stay clean for a bit, Bill, I pleaded inside, stay out of trouble, stay with Sheilagh in the country and don't do anything stupid. The Chaucer will take you – in two weeks' time . . .

A few nights later I got a call from my cousin. She told me: 'Bill had an accident driving back from London last night . . . swerved the car to avoid killing a stag, he says, and hit a tree head-on. He's OK, just rather shaken. But the car is a write-off. He could so easily have been killed. Anyway, he will call you later and tell you what happened himself . . .'

An hour later the phone rang again. This time it was Bill, sounding dazed and ashamed. Then the story came tumbling out. He had done it again, he had broken out. He was 'going stir-crazy cut off in Sussex', he told me. He had come up to London to collect his BMW – I guessed from the car park in Wapping where it had long been abandoned – at the same time arranging to meet Barbara Jones at a bar in Soho.

They had soon begun arguing about Bill's association with Alex. Much drink was consumed by Bill. Barbara had been the first to leave but she wisely and conscientiously returned to the bar to make sure Bill was not intending to drive, he told me. She had even grabbed his car keys, before flinging them into the gutter from where Bill had retrieved them. I could work the rest out for myself. Like a lunatic, he had headed back to Sussex behind the wheel of his powerful BMW in a drunken rage. He had crashed, been picked up by the police, breathalysed and arrested.

His car gone, he was now, it seemed, without means of further escape, and I was grateful at least for that. Perhaps the crash would shock him into accepting another shot at therapy, I remember thinking. Meanwhile, all I could hope for was that while back in the country he would at least stay clear of drugs. Yet for all I knew, Bill could find coke in a Sussex pub as easily as he had in Wandsworth, Fulham, Notting Hill or Wapping even. I remembered him saying to me once: 'You don't need to look far. Cocaine is everywhere. It finds you . . .'

It seemed to have found him in Sussex. Bill would sleep until midday, disappear to the local pub, then pace his bedroom all night, so Sheilagh would tell me later. He confessed later in his Priory diary that this, his own attempt at a 'white-knuckle detox', was a total failure. Sheilagh too by now had had enough. She rang to say gently that perhaps it would be better if we found somewhere else for him to stay in the days before the now imminent admission to the Chaucer. I couldn't argue – that she had agreed to have him at all had seemed like a miracle in the first place.

Bill caught the train up to London and, when Christy again refused to let him anywhere near our house, he checked once more into the Conrad Hotel at Chelsea Harbour for a last weekend of God knows what.

On a bright Monday morning, 6 March 2000, Christy took our daughters' battered little car to meet him outside the Conrad Hotel to take him to Ealing. Bill emerged blinking in the spring sunlight among the limos and glossy women heading for the Harbour Club. He looked like an asylum seeker. They set off for the Chaucer, Bill insisting on a last Guinness in a pub on the way. Christy could not stop him – Bill called it 'self-medication'.

For Bill it may have been a march to the scaffold. To us, the admission to the Chaucer was a last chance for survival. Christy was worried Bill would simply refuse to go in at all, or do a runner at the gates. He had ranted on the journey about: 'Crims and alkies . . . going on about their giros. I'm not like them . . . why are you bringing me here?'

In the end, Christy told me, my brother had gone through the Chaucer's battered doors with meek acceptance.

At first Bill called me on a payphone every couple of days. He told me he had been assigned to look after the garden alongside his new friend, John, the ex-con. He spoke of the tedium of the long alcohol-free evenings, the awful bleakness of facing up to what he had done to himself.

But by the end of his first month I began to detect a touching return of the 'old' Bill. He called me less, but when he did he sounded calmer and, if not exactly happy, more accepting of his fate.

One Saturday afternoon we talked for over an hour on the telephone, with Bill describing to me in detail how he had now discovered the clinic's library, and was re-reading the *Man in the Iron Mask* in the original French. He also mentioned watching a favourite film of his – Werner Herzog's *Aguirre, Wrath of God* – late into the night the evening before.

I had not heard Bill talk about films or books in several years. It was as if his personality were gradually seeping back into him, reviving his intellect, his enthusiasm, his self-respect.

And somehow he found enough sense of self-preservation to

dress up in a smart suit and get to Chichester for the court appearance on a charge of drink driving. With the support of a care-worker who accompanied him there and a letter from the Chaucer confirming he was in treatment for alcoholism, he telephoned afterwards to tell me he had escaped with a year's ban and a fine of £400.

A few weeks into Bill's admission, my daughter Maria and I went to visit him one Sunday afternoon. We found him in the small garden at the back of the hospital, dressed in faded jeans and an old black T-shirt, a radio blaring at his side while he weeded a flower bed with touching enthusiasm.

Bill seemed strangely contented, and fitter too, the muscles starting to reappear in his upper arms and torso, his jaw restored to its former firm line. Straightening up and grinning as we approached, he ran to fetch us rickety old formica chairs before offering Maria a cigarette and sitting down to chat.

After a few minutes he showed us around the garden, introducing us to John, his co-worker and fellow addict, before making us tea and fussing about like a suburban housewife in search of digestive biscuits. The whole scene was bizarre – broken people in a shabby yard at the back of an abandoned hospital holding a stilted conversation about last night's television programmes.

Yet so much more was going on: two men trying to resurrect their lives from a few square feet of grass and mud. I have never forgotten it. I left that afternoon filled with hope. Bill might really make it back this side of the looking glass.

The reports of his key workers were uniformly positive. I would see them four years later when I contacted Nick Charles for his reminiscences of Bill. They were like school reports, except 'marks' were given on such subjects as 'hobbies and pursuits', 'attitudes to addressing personal problems' and 'commitment to programme'.

Two weeks in, post-detoxification, Bill was judged to be 'getting on well with the other members and already feeling the therapeutic benefit of talking about his problems'. A month into the programme, and he was 'pleased his relationship with his wife is on the mend and this has cheered him up – a good level of commitment is being shown by Bill in all areas of the pro-gramme'.

It was all going fine. Then the moment would come when he would be allowed out for a 'home visit'.

23

As Easter Bank Holiday 2000 approached, Bill seemed increasingly cheerful. He was doing well, and the Chaucer was pleased with his progress. He was to be allowed out, he told me, to go home that weekend. Whose home? He was obviously looking forward to telling his 'wife' Alex about his transformation, and spending the weekend with her.

Then I got another call. Bill's tone was very different. He was angry: 'Would you blame me?' he asked inevitably. Alex had told him it was 'too soon' and that with Kevin in prison she could not cope if Bill 'went off the rails'. Max's condition was also deteriorating; the epileptic fits from which he had always suffered were now more frequent and severe. Her handicapped son was undergoing further tests both at Great Ormond Street in London and the John Radcliffe in Oxfordshire.

Bill was not sympathetic. If he could not see Alex, he decided, he would come and stay with us. For my own part, I felt he deserved some support from me for staying clean, as well as secretly welcoming the idea of having Bill back with my family.

When I told Christy he was not having any of it. 'I can't face it,' he said. 'You know what he's been like. How do we know he won't go back to using the moment he comes out?' I knew what was coming next. 'If Bill comes here, I'm off,' he said starkly. 'I'll take Joe to stay with my sister.' I did not have the strength left to put up much of a fight. I let it go, calling Bill to tell him that he was welcome to spend time with us, but that he would have to find somewhere else to sleep.

He did – with a woman doctor and former pethidine addict,

who had been in Promis with Bill five months earlier and who by some strange accident lived round the corner from our own house. I think it was Barbara Jones, who knew her independently, who arranged it. Our doctor-neighbour agreed to have him for the weekend.

On Good Friday 21 April 2000, Alex collected Bill by car from the Chaucer and brought him to me. His mood was hostile, edgy, and I could tell there had been trouble. We spent the afternoon playing with Joseph in the garden, along with Maria, who was with us for the weekend. Bill's attention was elsewhere, angry at Alex for being 'dumped'.

At about six o'clock I walked round with Bill to meet the doctor. She was having a dinner party and had already opened the champagne. Would Bill and I like a glass? I panicked.

'No, it is a bit early for me.'

Bill, of course, accepted the offer.

Half an hour later I left him, the pair of them now on their second bottle. Walking back, I wondered whether Christy had been right. Or maybe Bill was only drinking from a sense of rejection – not only by his girlfriend, but by his sister. Perhaps his lapse was my fault.

I heard nothing from Bill on the Saturday until the evening. Then he called to tell me he had had an argument with Alex over the phone. She had been with Lena, and in spite of his pleading had refused to see him. He had lost his temper. I did not need to ask if he had been drunk.

At seven o'clock in the morning on Easter Sunday, the telephone rang. It was Bill from the callbox at the end of our road. Could he come round? The doctor wanted him to leave her house, he said – he had upset all her friends at the dinner party and his behaviour the next day had not improved. He sounded pathetic. Christy was still asleep in bed, and Joseph was playing happily in front of the television. I said he could.

Two minutes later, Bill was on the doorstep, pale and unshaven. I brought him in and gave him tea and toast. Joseph was by now wrestling with his Easter present from me amid a pile of wrapping paper at Bill's feet. It was a bright-blue Thomas bicycle that needed to be put together.

Bill, never a handyman even when sober, tried his best with Christy's spanner set. Seeing him trying so hard to be normal suddenly struck me as incredibly sad. I wanted to cry.

Maria surfaced around an hour later. 'Can we all go to Brighton today?' she wanted to know. I went in to ask Christy and to explain to him why Bill was already in the house at such an hour. 'We can go,' he said, 'but he's not coming.'

Bill, Maria and I went round the corner to the coffee shop. Bill ordered a Cornish pasty, but ate only half of it. I broke the news that he couldn't come with us to Brighton:

'It would be too many of us in the car with Joe's baby seat and Maria as well, and anyway aren't you meant to check back in with the Chaucer by teatime?' I trailed off, unconvinced by my own excuse.

'I get it,' Bill snapped. 'You, my own flesh and blood . . .' I felt horrible, a Judas of a sister. Bill glared back at me. We walked back to the house in silence. Bill came in to get his jacket. 'Can you at least give me some money?' he demanded aggressively. I hesitated.

If I gave him cash, would he spend it on drink? I offered him a fiver and some pound coins out of my purse. Bill grabbed them before stalking off down the street. After he had gone, I noticed the toast I had made him had been discarded on the path uneaten. I was gripped with fear that he would go off on a bender – either that, or the clinic would boot him out anyway for boozing at all.

That evening I rang the Chaucer. Bill was there – thank God. He sounded calmer, saying to my surprise that he was glad to be back. He had talked to Alex, and apologised to her for being so aggressive. He realised how much she had to put up with at the moment.

I asked if the clinic had noticed he had been drinking. 'I don't think so,' he said. 'They expect it, don't they, when they let you out?'

His key worker's weekly report for 30 April read: 'Bill has not experienced any problems this week that he requires to discuss. He has had a pleasant week and his relationship with close family continues to improve.' He had another five weeks of the programme to go.

Bill lasted another five days. At lunchtime on 5 May 2000 he suddenly discharged himself, claiming he had had a phone call from 'work' saying he was wanted back urgently. There was no work. Bill had left *The Times* over a year before.

'Bill came to see me in my office before he left,' so Nick Charles recalled five years later. 'He looked terrific – really fit and well. But from experience I knew he wasn't ready to leave, not psychologically recovered enough to cope with outside again.

'I tried to persuade him to stay even if only for another couple of weeks. Then Bill said to me: "I've been to your lectures, Nick, and listened to all you have to say. You describe that amazing high that drinkers get from alcohol. Well, I get that. The only other thing in life that has ever given me that is the incredible buzz I get from being in the newsroom. I want that back. I want it back so much. That is why I have to leave . . ." '

'Two men in a BMW came to take him away,' so Nick Charles recalled, 'One of them had been several times before.' He had no idea who he was. Whatever had been cooked up, Bill seemed to be back on with Alex.

I confess to being relieved at the time – at the idea of them together again. For all my reservations, I could not forbid the relationship – like our own father might have disapproved of some unsuitable partner when Bill and I were in our teens. Alex was loyal and caring against impossible odds. She had visited him in the Chaucer; I knew that. She had said she would have him back if he stayed clean. Maybe, maybe, that would be enough.

And in the weeks after his self-discharge from the Chaucer he was functioning much better – as far as I could tell. The ordinary things – like money, somewhere to live, that there might be a day after tomorrow – had begun to enter the space in his head where booze and drugs had seemed to have taken up permanent residence. With sobriety came the realisation of the facts.

Bill was broke. If he got his hands on money, I was concerned it would soon be heading the way of his local cocaine dealer. But above anything else, Bill needed somewhere to live. I could not take him in. Christy was still adamant.

I met Barbara Jones to discuss what to do. She of course disapproved of Alex, loathed any mention of the Hanleys. I suspect now that Barbara knew more about what was really going on than I did. But she remained committed to saving my brother, and between us we tried to come up with a practical plan.

Barbara had long shared a bank manager with Bill, a man named Alan Green. She now told him to expect a call from me, leaving the two of us to talk about how a cleaned-up Bill might function financially. Alan Green, miraculously it seemed to me, produced a timely insurance policy on the now long-ago sold house in Wiseton Road, which it appeared could now be cashed in for £17,000. I told Barbara, who advised me strongly not to tell Bill about this apparent lifeline until we could be sure he was really clean.

I disagreed. Bill's solution to financial worries was just to drink more – he would surely do it again. So I told him directly about Alan Green's happy discovery. That sort of money was enough for him to rent somewhere to live and buy food until he was well enough, perhaps, to start working again. He was overjoyed – I had saved him. He promised, promised that this was the turning point. Barbara was convinced meanwhile that Bill's relief was more than partly due to being able to finance his habit. I could only pray that she would be proved wrong.

Bill, as always, wanted Alex to live with him. She refused, until she could see the 'staying off drugs' would last. Bill meanwhile had money to spend. The two of them spent several days trawling flats, location, location, location, in the Wandsworth Bridge and Fulham area, not far from my family home across the river and very close indeed to various members of the Hanley clan.

Two weeks later they found one that Bill, if not happy with, at least had no objections to. The address was No. 3 Anselm Road – a ground floor flat in a house just off the North End Road.

I still remember the first time I went there to visit Bill. The place looked cheerful enough that morning, with the strong light of summer falling on the white-painted walls, wooden work-surfaces and shiny-resined floorboards of the typical Fulham flat. Aimed at the classic estate agent's target – a single man spending his time as ludicrously advertised on the local billboards, 'in the surrounding vibrant bars and restaurants' – the remainder of the property consisted of a tiny kitchen, bathroom and bedroom adjoining the main living space.

I was reminded for a moment of the last time I had left my brother like this, in a room rearranging his belongings, all those years before in Oxford. A large mirror above the marble fireplace reflected my brother's sleep-rejuvenated face, eyes clear, his skin freckled as it had been in childhood.

Bill's first few weeks in Anselm Road were encouraging. As far as I knew, he was off both drink and drugs – now even talking optimistically both about going back to *The Times,* as well as approaching the *Telegraph* for work. He looked well enough, but there was something else in his expression, a mixture of bafflement and terror.

I thought I could do this bit – make optimistic noises about the future, chivvy him about getting a job, buy Flash and hoover bags, behave in fact just like our mother might have done. We talked at length about what he should be doing, writing CVs and sending off letters. But all he actually achieved each day was to get himself up, watch daytime television and, very occasionally, clean up around him and get some shopping in. Each day he would phone me – going on for hours about inane soaps and chat shows.

He was living the life of a layabout undergraduate, heading for finals without having done a stroke of work, knowing that he was the author of his own looming disastrous denouement – yet observing himself doing so with a certain wry amusement. Any talk about getting a job, getting back to the 'buzz of a newsroom', had evaporated. No colleagues, with one brave exception, had been calling him.

I would wearily go over and do what I could. After a month it was clear that his health was again deteriorating, with minor complaints such as eye infections and inexplicable cuts and grazes that would not heal. After one bout of conjunctivitis, I tried to persuade Bill to sign up with a local GP. But my brother was having none of it.

Bill was drinking. It was obvious. He wanted no intervention by judgmental doctors or anyone else. My pleas were clearly those of yet another nagging woman. His life was shrinking to a rubbish-strewn patch of west London, shuffling daily to an off-licence, the aptly named 'Hair of the Dog' in North End Road market, and back round the corner to his flat.

Food was an irrelevance – refuelling himself instead on litres and litres of Stolichnaya vodka. He had given up pretending, the flat was full of bottles. I went round one day to clear them out. Bill was slumped with what I thought was an uneaten pizza on the floor in front of him. It turned out to be a platter of Marlboro cigarette butts, hundreds of them, obsessively arranged in a spiral like a miniature crop circle. He caught me staring at it and a glimpse of the old Bill suddenly slipped through the wooden façade:

'It's a still life . . . what do you think?'

I smiled, in spite of myself, and he smiled back. We were kids again making a joke at the absurdities of life. Except we were not kids. Bill was almost fifty years old. His health was declining rapidly, new symptoms appeared daily – stiffness in his back, neck and limbs. I guessed this was due both to the weakness of his muscles and his general lack of movement. Occasionally there would also be some more urgent crisis such as breathlessness, dizziness or bouts of uncontrollable coughing.

A few weeks later came the call I had been both expecting and dreading: 'I'm really scared, Clare. I don't know what's wrong with me, but my legs won't work. I think I need a doctor . . .'

24

The pretty young Asian GP at the Fulham Road surgery gave Bill an appraising yet softly sympathetic glance. Then she turned to Christy and me, perched tensely on our chairs on either side of Bill like ushers in a courtroom. She addressed all her remarks to us. It was as if Bill were a child.

'He may be suffering from depression . . . he's certainly in a bad way,' she said. 'My problem is what we can do about it. NHS resources in cases like his are notoriously restricted, and what there is available tends to get directed towards adolescents.'

I looked at Bill and felt terrified. We had seen the nurse a few minutes earlier when the GP had routinely requested that Bill be weighed and have his blood pressure taken. The scales read just under nine and a half stone. Bill was six foot two. He had looked gaunt enough when he was 2 stone heavier. Now he was skeletal.

'We could try and get him a psychiatric assessment,' she continued. 'But he would have to be sober on the day of the appointment or they won't touch him. Otherwise you could try taking him to the Warwick Road Clinic to ask for a referral to an addiction treatment centre . . .'

I knew about Warwick Road, a walk-in NHS unit in west London. Alex had already tried taking Bill there. But he had walked out halfway through the afternoon, bored by sitting in a waiting-room full of addicts and alcoholics he still did not recognise as having anything in common with himself.

'But your brother could get lucky and get a referral from there – either to an NHS unit, or possibly even privately,' the doctor continued brightly. I looked at Bill again. His face was blank. If anything it bore an expression of mild amusement. He had said virtually nothing throughout except mutter mild obscenities.

Bill suddenly groaned; he was clutching his stomach. The doctor looked alarmed and took him behind some curtains. 'I think we better get your brother into hospital straightaway,' she said on their return. Drunk or sober, they would have to take him now.

Christy managed to get him the short distance to St Stephens Hospital on the Fulham Road. I got a cab to pick up our son from nursery school. The A&E assessment nurse was coldly efficient, so Christy told me later that evening. Bill was suffering from internal bleeding from the stomach, they said, probably a perforated ulcer, meriting an immediate admission. Christy had left Bill grinning broadly as two Australian male nurses whisked him off somewhere within. My brother was seriously ill, but I felt, as always, relieved to have the responsibility lifted off me by professionals. At least I would be able to sleep that night knowing someone was taking care of him.

Bill stayed in hospital for the next ten days, during which time we took it in turns to visit him. Alex went too – as did her mother Bridget. She always had a soft spot for Bill. Danny McGrory, his old newsroom colleague, also went to visit, lifting Bill's mood and inspiring him to talk of getting back to work again.

Our daughter Katy also went in to see her uncle, prompting much envy from Bill's fellow patients about the presence at his bedside of such an attractive young girl. Maria, her identical twin, came with me a few days later, causing even further confusion on the men's surgical ward.

While we were there that afternoon, a junior house doctor came by, glanced briefly at Bill's chart, and said:

'Your brother is doing very well, Mrs Campbell. He can be discharged very shortly.'

'Oh no, please,' I replied, 'if you send him back to that flat again . . . You don't understand, it will all start all over again . . .'

'What will, Mrs Campbell?' The doctor spoke patronisingly, as if to some difficult child.

'Don't you understand why he is here?' I protested. 'He's

drinking, and doing drugs all the time . . . he's destroying himself. I hoped you would help . . .'

'Help, Mrs Campbell? I don't think your brother needs any help. He certainly hasn't asked for any. In fact, he strikes me as a very competent man. He has been telling me about his work as a journalist. I am sure a man who could look after himself in Bosnia can manage to make himself the odd plate of baked beans on toast.'

'Would you at least arrange for him to see a drugs counsellor before you discharge him?' I asked angrily.

'I can't do that, I am afraid. Not unless he asks for a visit himself. Anyway, they only come around once a fortnight.'

'When is their next visit?'

'You've missed it . . . It was last week. So it looks like your brother will be discharged before the next one.'

'Don't you understand what I am telling you?' I was almost shrieking by now. 'He will die if he goes back to that flat.'

The doctor cut across me, his eyes hard through his black-framed glasses. 'Your brother's body is mended now. What goes on in his mind is none of my business.'

Four days later, Bill was discharged. It was a warm July in London. Bill went back to the permanent twilight of Anselm Road, the curtains always drawn, the television always on. His only visitors now were myself, Christy, and the ever-loyal Danny, whose friendship for Bill went beyond that of any other colleague.

Alex understandably kept her distance. She had enough trouble in her life already. Bill's attention was turned on me. I myself could hardly bear to take his ranting, pleading phone calls, the confused messages left on the answer machine alternating between rage, obsession and self-pity. Then quite suddenly the calls stopped. This silence was worse and far more frightening. Now I called him instead. The phone just rang and rang. I sensed there was no more fight left in him. It was as if Bill had given up.

He himself wrote in his Priory confessional: 'I pile up unopened bills in a dark corner of the flat. I won't open the door or answer the telephone even though I know it is probably a friend. Going to the shops has become an ordeal, a paranoid nightmare. The larder is empty.'

And he added this – something I myself suspected all along – 'I think a part of me actually enjoyed the chaos – a sort of dark joke. I watched my own disintegration with a kind of detached amusement.'

There was another admission to St Stephens a few weeks later. Bill had collapsed again. Not his stomach this time, it was his legs. Somehow Christy and I got him from the flat, borne on our shoulders the short distance to the hospital like a battlefield casualty. We dropped him into a wheelchair we found in an alleyway. It was midday. The wait to see anyone was interminable. Around four o' clock, he saw the A&E nurse.

'What's wrong?' she asked, 'have you been drinking?'

'And some other stuff,' said Bill.

The wait went on. This was going nowhere. Christy and I, on our own volition, wheeled him out on to the street past startled shoppers and round to the back of the hospital where a 'psychiatric unit' was signposted. A security man stopped us – 'You can't bring him in here'. Desperate, I barged past and found some inhabited office. The woman duty psychiatrist was alarmed, but pleasant enough. She examined Bill in the corridor. She told us that she could do nothing for my brother because he was clearly drunk. 'Make an appointment – it would have to be sometime in October. Oh, and of course, he will have to be sober.'

Bill was lolling, unable to walk. With great reluctance, the Casualty nurse at last took him back in her care. I went off, barely functioning myself, to collect Joseph from school. Christy waited in the hospital for several more hours before returning home exhausted and despairing. He told me he had finally left Bill sitting in Casualty, still raving, still waiting to be seen by a doctor. From nine in the evening onwards, I called Bill's number at the flat, at last getting a reply at around midnight.

The hospital had discharged him half an hour before. God alone knows how he had got himself home.

25

There was one last line of hope. In fact, it was Barbara Jones's idea. Go back to *The Times* management and see if they would fund another stab at rehab. We had a new and persuasive case to make.

There had been talk during Bill's earlier brushes with addiction professionals of what he had seen in Beirut or the Balkans having contributed to his self-immolation. I remembered his account of the Bosnian village full of crucified men, of how he had slugged back the wine as he told me through gritted teeth what he had seen. I remembered him during the Rosemary West trial in Winchester– the horror all bottled up inside.

I had not yet read his Priory account (Bill had yet to write it) of the 'images of blood and atrocity that were too vivid to mention or share', or of the breakfast slivovitz and 'opium tea' with which he had numbed the pain of Bosnia. He had called it, no doubt with some therapy-speak acquired along the way, 'self-medication'.

Bill had signed himself into the Chaucer as suffering from 'post-traumautic stress' after spending 'twenty-five years as a war correspondent'. He had declared something similar, I would later discover, to his therapists in Arizona. It might have been a diversion, but I had no better explanation at the time for what might be going on in his head. All I knew was that he had been to the wars and reported them brilliantly. And at least by saying his condition was as a result of this, my brother was clinging to some kind of macho personal dignity.

He had been physically injured in Sarajevo and *The Times* had paid for the treatment to repair his damaged leg. It was a simple enough case to argue that they should do the same again for his mind. I asked the Managing Editor of *The Times* if Bill's former employers would pay for at least a psychiatric assessment. Barbara Jones added her ever-forceful voice. We cajoled, we threatened and we begged. *The Times* management at last agreed. The company doctor would see him first.

One morning in August 2000, Christy reversed our daughter's dented Peugeot into a parking space between two large glossy diplomatic cars in Knightsbridge. Bill sat muttering to himself in the passenger seat, smelling of alcohol. I leant forward between the seats to grasp his hand, looking up at the Harrods building where our mother had taken us as children for a half-term treat.

Opposite was a terrace of white stucco houses. One of them contained the consulting rooms of Dr Gordon, *The Times* personnel department medical adviser. He had telephoned me the previous day offering an appointment. All was brass plaques, soft carpets and cut flowers. He greeted Bill warmly and invited Christy and me to relax in the elegant waiting room awash with glossy magazines while he talked to my brother alone. Please Bill, I willed him silently, don't screw this up. Don't rage, or boast, and above all don't lie.

About twenty minutes into the interview, the door of the consulting room suddenly opened. Dr Gordon came out, tall and imposing, his face serious and bearing a slightly quizzical expression.

'I wonder if you would mind stepping in for a moment, Mrs Campbell . . . and your husband, too, if he wouldn't mind?'

I was falling into a pit. Perhaps it might still be OK. Maybe I could apologise for whatever discourtesy my brother had been displaying, rescue the situation in some way before it turned into another smash-up.

'I am confused,' Dr Gordon announced, 'as to why, when your brother flatly denies having a problem with alcohol, you have brought him to see me. He says he hasn't had a drink for a week, and that he is not in need of any assistance.'

I looked at Bill pleadingly from the other side of the room, and could see him, head on one side, ruffling up in his chair like a cockerel ready for a fight.

'Bill,' I said despairingly, 'Tell the truth. That you have been drinking. You wanted to come here. I didn't make you . . .'

Always angrier when he had been made to feel guilty, Bill snarled: 'OK, OK . . . so I have had a drink and yes, I have been doing drugs too, cocaine mostly, and other stuff. So what?'

Dr Gordon stepped in. In a quiet tone I have never forgotten he said: 'You do realise, Bill, that if you carry on like this you are going to die? Do you want that to happen?'

For a moment a look of absolute terror flashed across my brother's face before a Lear-like fury took its place.

'YES, I FUCKING DO,' he roared, before, his voice breaking now, he sobbed: 'You don't understand. It's too late. I've nothing left. I've got to get out of it . . .'

I made a move to go towards him to comfort him, but Dr Gordon raised a hand in warning, before speaking again: 'I don't think you mean that, Bill, and I am going to disregard it. I think you do want to get well. On the basis of that . . .' He turned towards me and said quietly, 'I am going to write to the managing editor of *The Times* today and recommend that we fund Bill for a short stay in the Priory Hospital where he will undergo a short course of treatment. Should his condition deteriorate before his admission, please call me immediately. You have my number?'

He looked at me over the top of his glasses for a moment, while I simply thought: 'Thank God.'

Then he stood up and offered his hand to Bill: 'Good luck.'

Bill hesitated, obviously ashamed of himself, before shambling away as fast as he could in the direction of the front door. Dr Gordon hastily waved away my gratitude, 'Not at all, not at all. I don't like to see a man throw away his talents . . .'

Outside Christy leant against the car door, lighting a cigarette in relief as Bill climbed in past him, still mumbling resentfully: 'Fucking doctors are all the same. Think they know it all . . .'

Getting into the car I touched his shoulder, looking at him

steadfastly, willing him to take this warning seriously. 'Bill, you heard what Dr Gordon said? That you are killing yourself . . . ?'

'He didn't mean that. He was just trying to scare me . . .'

26

Bill and I sat huddled in the car together staring up at the 1960s red-brick house, Galsworthy Lodge, the drug and alcohol unit of the Priory Hospital in Roehampton on the edge of Richmond Park where I had brought him for an initial assessment. Getting an admission to the NHS/charity-funded Chaucer had taken weeks of anguish, but, as with the earlier referral to Promis, getting Bill into privately funded rehab had moved with well-oiled efficiency.

Postponing our moment of entry for as long as possible, I noticed how cosily suburban the building seemed, with its little shrubs and white net curtains at the windows – *Abigail's Party* at the heart of the addiction industry.

A gaggle of fashionable-looking people lurked in the rhododendrons nearby, indulging in a post-therapy fag. Cigarettes and coffee were just about tolerated here, but nothing stronger.

Bill had also been offered this dress circle ticket to redemption – if only he was sensible enough to take it. I watched Bill's fingers grasping the handle on the glove compartment – the nicotine stains and the jagged uncut nails.

During the drive there, he had talked of finding it hard to leave the flat, to talk to anyone apart from me, particularly over the phone. He also spoke of experiencing strange recurrent dreams so vivid he found it difficult to separate them from reality. He said he was terrified he might be going mad.

I wanted to reach out, to tell him it would all be all right, that I would take care of him. But if this last, last chance was about anything, it was about Bill being made able to look after himself.

'I suppose we had better go in?' I said.

Bill did not answer straightaway. I guessed he was aware, as I was, of the oddness of the drama we now found ourselves in, wondering by what route our sibling lives had brought us here.

'Would you come in and see this guy with me?' Bill asked suddenly.

'It's just that I don't always remember everything . . . You can tell him stuff too, about the way I behave sometimes . . .'

'This guy', I knew, was the counsellor who had agreed to see Bill, to assess whether or not the Priory could help him. I knew how much Bill would hate having to be the supplicant.

'Of course.'

'Thank you so much . . . for everything,' Bill said abruptly and, half-turning in his seat, squeezed both arms around me and said: 'I love you very much. You know that, don't you?'

A few minutes later we were sitting opposite a smiling, bearded man in his forties. He seemed kind and friendly, himself imbued with the born-again zeal of the recovered addict that I was beginning to find so familiar. Opening up a large blue and white folder, he announced: 'Before I can tell you whether we can help you, Bill, I need to ask you a few questions . . .'

I sensed Bill wincing at the man's placatory tone, the too-soon familiarity of the use of his first name. Bill loathed the whole business of therapy, with its platitudinous psychobabble – of having to place himself in the power of yet another hierarchy of those he regarded as fools and charlatans. He had been to this place before as a sceptical journalist – two years later he was being assessed for his own suitability to enter the 'celebrity asylum'.

He hated being told anything he did was wrong. He hated men with beards. He said he hated life; this man was trying to save it.

Reluctant at first to allow a relative, however close, to share the privacy of the confessional, Bill's insistence that he wanted me there finally worked on his interrogator. I took a seat on a low chair in the corner behind Bill, and waited for the session to begin.

The counsellor then proceeded with a detailed 'history-taking' – at what age Bill had first tasted alcohol, how it had made him feel, and when he first became aware that he might have a problem with it. He was asked to give specific examples of his behaviour after drinking, embarrassments, sexual misdeanours, attacks of nausea, amnesia or total blackout. What shocked me most were not so much my brother's lurid accounts of teenage acid trips, vodka binges or cocaine nights, as the large chunks of our shared experience that had gone missing altogether. Ages, names of close relatives, whole time frames of our family history were either muddled or simply not there at all.

Intermittently Bill would glance over in my direction for reassurance, frequently calling on me to fill in the blanks. So we continued for over an hour while I prayed that Bill would not, as so often before, do something to smash it all up. Somehow, I did not think Bill would. Not today.

After the assessment was over, Bill and I drove in reflective silence to a café not far away in Barnes. Bill announced he was hungry. I remember thinking this must be a good sign. He had not talked of wanting food for several months. Ordering a toasted sandwich with his coffee, he lit a cigarette, hands trembling and, leaning forwards across the table to me, said quietly: 'I realise this is my last chance, Clare . . . I've got to do this, haven't I, or I'm finished . . .'

Later that day he called Alex, told her he had had the assessment, pleaded with her for another chance. She said she would need real proof that this time Bill meant what he said.

A few days later, Bill was admitted to the Priory. Alex drove him there. He really seemed determined this time to make it work. His friend from Bosnia, the BBC reporter Fergal Keane, came to see him, providing Bill with the kind of support only another recovering addict could offer. Sometimes Fergal brought his son, Daniel, then aged four – like Joseph – along with him.

Bill enjoyed their visits, talked of getting the two boys together when he came out: his nephew and Fergal's son. He said having Joe made him feel better about not having been a father himself. He suddenly seemed a lot more hopeful. I talked to my own editor at the *Daily Mail*. She knew Bill's professional reputation as a reporter and writer, and had bought in a piece of his from *The Times* in the past. She was encouraging. There was talk of giving him a features job.

Bill was thrilled. He would come out of rehab, work hard, stay clean, win Alex back. He was optimistic again. Three weeks into the admission he wrote: 'Admitting I was powerless over my addictions was not difficult – I have known as much for some time. The problem was I didn't care – oblivion seemed preferable to life . . .' Now, it seemed, life might be preferable.

27

Arriving at Galsworthy Lodge one Saturday afternoon, my daughter Maria and I were surprised by the celebratory atmosphere of the place. We had come to see Bill, a sanctioned visit for relatives of addicts to attend a group therapy session – an opportunity to address the family's feelings about how addictive behaviour had impacted on their own lives.

I had imagined a few tearful relatives sitting hunched in a therapy room, with lots of tissues close to hand. Instead we were now ushered through the small hallway into a room packed with people talking, laughing, smoking and generally enjoying themselves. A well-stocked buffet lunch was spread out on a table placed down one wall – a detoxifying spread of green salads, dips and wheat-free bread. There was no wine, of course, the Priory's one concession to stimulants being a single flask of Lavazza coffee, siphoned up within minutes.

French windows on the opposite side opened on to a garden where trees and a few climbing shrubs provided shade for those of the congregation jostling outside in the early September sunshine. Taking our plates and coffee with us, Maria and I sat mesmerised on some rickety green garden seats. It was more like a summer drinks party than a gritty family truth or dare. Among the faces that floated by were several I recognised professionally, an actor here, a model there (including one I had once interviewed).

I had to scan the crowd several times before eventually locating Bill, talking animatedly to someone in the shrubbery. Bill was standing tall and upright again. His companion, who was a short, middle-aged man, dressed in smart, casual clothes, had to tilt backwards to look up at him. Both were laughing and obviously liked one another.

Moments later I saw the red-headed model again, looking pale and agitated, as she peered anxiously over in our direction. 'Just a moment,' Bill promised me and went over to chat to her. On his return he grinned broadly, his handsome face reflecting both the weight gain and the semi-miraculous return of physical health.

'It's OK,' he said. 'She recognised you and thought you were here spying for the *Mail* – said she was frightened that you might get straight on the phone and say you had seen her here . . .' I was here to see my sick brother. It was a textbook example of the addict's mantra: 'Everything is about me'.

We were all summoned upstairs where – after being divided up, each with our token addict, into groups of about twelve – we took our places for the real purpose of the afternoon: group family therapy.

Everyone was reticent at first. Then gradually the visiting relatives began to summon enough courage to start talking. The young wife of Leonard, the man I had seen talking to Bill earlier, opened by telling her husband, a wealthy businessman, how it had made her feel to come home from shopping one morning to find him ignoring his two baby sons while he snorted a line of coke off their coffee table.

Leonard cut across her, his defence running along the predictable line that his wife didn't understand 'what it was like to be him'. The counsellor pointed out that this was the purpose of our getting together that afternoon, and that perhaps if Leonard would allow his wife to finish speaking, he might for once find out what it was like to be her.

Suddenly a well-dressed, attractive woman in her mid-fifties launched into a lengthy tirade against her son, Henry, an elegantly gaunt and floppy-haired young man in his early twenties who spoke in the slightly petulant drawl of an old Etonian.

Henry, his mother told us, had been taking drugs since the age of fifteen, starting with cannabis, and graduating to heroin and cocaine by the time he reached his A levels. He had already been in rehab on several occasions, each attempt at staying clean lasting no longer than a few weeks.

His mother, Marion, said she had now reached a point of despair, and having twice broken into his flat and found him unconscious, was now terrified of losing him for ever.

Henry now began to answer his mother back, saying he was sorry that his behaviour had this effect on her, but that what he did with his life was no longer any of her business.

It was only when Marion began describing what thoughts rushed through her mind when Henry did not pick up his phone, the imagined scene of her son's dead body, that Bill suddenly spoke for the first time:

'I know why he doesn't answer your call,' he said.

There was a silence as the room waited for my brother to continue.

'I recognise that feeling . . . I hear the phone ringing. I know it's my sister and that she's probably worried about me. But when I'm doing a line, it's just . . . well, an irritant.'

So that was it. My concern, my worry, my terror for Bill's very life was a minor obstacle in the indulgence of his habit. Compassion drained from me. I wanted to explode with the full force of the built-up fury and resentment of the last two years.

But I did not need to. As I started to open my mouth to speak, an angry buzz swept round the table as every 'carer' in that room began simultaneously to rebel. Bill's remark had apparently encapsulated all they most resented both about addiction itself and the attitude of their own unrepentant sons, daughters, siblings and spouses. Now the families had had just about as much as they could stand. It was their turn to go on the offensive.

Leonard's wife again led the attack, asking Henry if he was aware how selfish he sounded. Then she asked him if he had ever lain awake at night wondering whether someone he loved were alive or dead, and had he any idea what that felt like?

Henry turned crimson, mumbling something incomprehensible into his lap while Leonard started to nudge his wife to back off. The counsellor looked nervous and, like a chat-show host realising his guests have spent too long in the green room, struggled desperately to regain control.

So we continued back and forth for another hour, although I began to doubt, the longer and more bitterly it went on, the real value of this attempted mutual understanding by the addicted and the 'clean'. Could Bill have any real comprehension of my worries for him – any more than I could imagine myself in his head when he was 'out of it'? I did not believe so.

Afterwards, as we said goodbye to one another, we talked briefly of Dr Gordon's proposed visit to the Priory the following week. Bill looked and sounded well, almost back to his old self. I told him I was certain Dr Gordon would report his obvious improvement to *The Times*, and that it would not be too long before he was back at work.

Bill looked anxiously back at me, apparently unconvinced.

'Do you really think so?' he asked plaintively. 'I'm not so sure . . .'

Pulling down the drive a few minutes later, I caught sight of Bill in my driving mirror, still standing staring after us. For a moment I had the strongest instinct to turn the car back round and return to him. At that moment, Maria wound down the passenger window, waving back at her uncle as she lit a cigarette. Bill smiled and turned back for the house.

The moment of urgency had passed.

28

Waking that morning, 7 December 2000, the day of Bill's funeral, a string of words floated into my head: 'I don't want to be standing at Bill's graveside with everyone saying they wished they had done more'.

It was the voice of Barbara Jones, talking to me when we first discussed our last pleading approach to *The Times* four months before. Well, we had done that, I thought. It hadn't worked. I felt angry, wanting to lash out at someone. But who to blame? Not his employers – they in the end had been more than honourable. Post-traumatic stress – what he had seen and experienced as a war reporter? Perhaps. Drugs – Kevin Hanley – or Bill himself? Too difficult to untangle all of that. All that mattered right now was that Bill was gone. Meanwhile, I had to face the funeral. That was going to be a war zone of its own.

Arriving at the crematorium in south London, Christy had not finished parking the car before my cousin Sheilagh approached, thrusting a briefcase at me and saying, 'Here, you must have this. Bill left it with me when he stayed.'

I looked down. It was not an attractive object. Made of dark-grey transparent plastic, the case bore a crest, a small shark cruising between gold-embossed letters. To me it conjured up a world of Rolex watches and gold medallions – of 'Ken Masters' in *Howard's Way*.

I didn't want to carry it into the chapel. Putting the briefcase into the back of our ancient Volvo, I wondered for a moment why Bill would be carrying round this strange case full of documents at a time when he did not even know what day it was.

A few moments later I had forgotten Sheilagh and was in a sea of faces – relatives, colleagues, friends of Bill's I had not seen for years, tentatively offering condolences, murmuring commiserations, or silently hugging me close. It was overwhelming. Turning, I saw Ruth, Bill's ex-wife, and her sister, Margaret, his first girlfriend. I went to move towards them, catching sight as I did so of Alex, dramatic in white shirt and black overcoat, huge sunglasses covering her face. Beside her, supporting her by the elbow, stood her sister-in-law, Lena, the wife of Kevin Hanley.

Keeping them in my sightline as I greeted Ruth, I began to see how complex the politics of this funeral were about to become. There was Barbara Jones, too, arriving a few minutes afterwards, her son, Matthew, and his new wife, Maria, standing protectively at her side.

There was no grieving widow present that cold December morning. Bill instead had one ex-wife and two former girlfriends at his funeral. They hated each other. I was the sister, not the adjudicator. He had loved Alex, or told me that he did. Bill would have wanted Alex to be here. Whatever I privately thought, I had to put Bill's feelings first.

Conscious of Barbara's stern gaze, I walked over towards Alex and mumbled some sort of condolence. Alex was very pale, her expression distraught, her clothes far less glossy than I had ever seen her wearing before. We talked briefly before my daughter Katy called me to say we should go in – the chapel was filling up and the service was about to start.

Father Michael, the Catholic priest officiating, spoke of Bill's talent, his humour, how loved he had been. He described his addiction, or 'problems' as he discreetly put it, being the result of what he called an 'increasingly troubled life'.

Glancing behind me I saw Ruth, Alex and Barbara, points of a triangle, now strategically situated around the chapel as far away from each other as possible.

The ceremony was short and dignified. Pat Bishop read a dispatch of Bill's from Bosnia. Christy said a few words. My twin daughters, Katy and Maria, stood on either side of me, supporting me, understanding my crippling sense of loss. There was some music – Schubert, which Christy chose, and 'Sympathy for the Devil' by the Stones, upon which I insisted. Bill would have liked the Stones.

Immediately the service was over the factions split off again. Bill's affairs with women had been complicated enough when he was alive, and his death had not made them any simpler. Although the majority of the guests, including Alex, followed us back to our house in Wandsworth for the wake, Ruth, in the company of several of Bill's oldest friends from school and university, diverted to a Streatham pub. They were always loyal to Ruth. They never showed up afterwards.

Barbara Jones meanwhile disappeared somewhere with a group of reporters from the *Mail on Sunday* – to stormily appear at our house much later, unhappy at Alex's presence. I don't think they had ever met before that day. It was funny really. Bill would have enjoyed it. At least there was passion amid the grief. I just felt numb.

I found comfort in the company of hacks who packed out our little kitchen and downstairs room. Their stories displayed their affection and admiration for Bill, his humour, his charm, his talent. Their words brought his presence back so strongly that several times I caught myself scanning the room, half expecting to see him.

Later in the afternoon, I talked to Father Michael about Bill's anguish before he died. The priest nodded at the distinguished company that filled our house. 'Ah, but Clare – look around you,' he said. 'Your parents would have been so proud. You should take comfort from that.' My parents, I knew, would have preferred their son to be alive and well.

Much later into the evening, Danny McGrory took me to one side. 'It was you, Clare, not Alex or Barbara or any of the rest of them,' he said. 'You were the one he always returned to, the one who was there whatever happened.' I hoped so, hoped with all my heart that Bill knew that was true.

Bill's memorial service was held at St Bride's, the journalists' church just off Fleet Street, on 28 March 2001, four months after his death. If the funeral had been mainly about the private Bill –

his former wife and quarrelling girlfriends – the memorial celebrated his professional side with the formal accolades of his colleagues and tributes from his friends and former bosses at *The Times* and the BBC.

It was clear from the cast list that Bill had made a substantial mark in his passing. Danny McGrory, and Jim Naughtie, his former colleague at the *Today* programme, gave personal and often very funny reminiscences of the pleasure of working alongside him. The BBC reporter Fergal Keane, who had been with him at the wars and supported Bill through his treatment at the Priory, chose a reading from Corinthians; and Peter Stothard, the then editor of *The Times*, read 'A Disused Shed in County Wexford' by Derek Mahon, an appropriate and moving epitaph for a former foreign correspondent.

Looking around St Bride's that morning, I remembered Father Michael's words to me at the funeral. The church was packed with journalists, broadcasters and writers, colleagues who Bill, lost in the paranoia of addiction, had convinced himself had cut him out of their lives.

Bill had believed his career was over, and worse, that no one cared. Yet if he could only have been there, witnessed for himself just how greatly he was loved as well as respected, it might have given him the reason to want to stay alive.

I did not see Alex or Lena Hanley in the congregation. Nor did I spot them as we spilled out of the crowded church to join Danny McGrory and the rest of Bill's friends afterwards in El Vino's, the journalists' bar nearby in Blackfriars. But they had certainly both been there – others had seen them. I read it for myself in *The Times* court and social page the following morning.

PART THREE

29

It was almost two years since my brother's death when the Operation Extend revelations came tumbling out, with the conclusion of the last of the trials on 12 June 2002. There it was for the world to see – the biggest drugs bust in British legal history. The press reports hit me in slow motion – I suppose I was still half numb with grief. Bit by bit I began to realise the significance of it all. Up to then everything about the 'Wright Organisation' – about the reasons for the Customs raid on my house, about Kevin Stephen Hanley – was secret. Not knowing was horrible enough as conspiracy theories flashed through my head and I raged against those I considered were responsible. Now I knew a lot more. It was as if I were blinking awake after a long confused dream. It was as if I were suddenly visited by an overwhelming sense of curiosity. What I was not prepared for was the sheer scale of it.

'Customs officers have smashed a massive cocaine smuggling ring in an investigation they describe as "without parallel" in Britain, it can be reported for the first time today,' said the *Evening Standard*.

'The gang leader Brian Wright can be named today as Britain's most wanted drug smuggler,' the story continued. 'Nicknamed "Uncle" or "The Milkman" because he always delivers, Wright escaped to Northern Cyprus which has no extradition treaty with Britain. But among those in prison serving major sentences are his 34-year-old son, also named Brian Wright, his foremost lieutenant Kevin Hanley, and Ronaldo Soares, his link with the Colombian cocaine barons of Medellín.

'A senior Customs source said: "It was probably the most sophisticated and successful global cocaine organisation ever to target the UK. Wright is a menace, continues to be a menace and we want to catch him." '

Where was Bill in all of this? What had he really done? Was he aware of the size of the conspiracy and, if so, what might that knowledge have done to his mind? Was he so frightened by what he knew, even if he had only the scrappiest, drug-addled comprehension, that any attempt to save his life was doomed all along? He had told Dr Gordon, *The Times* doctor, that he 'wanted to die'. That it was 'too late'. What had he meant?

There was not much to go on. The Customs' press release and the flurry of news reports that followed posed as many questions as they gave answers. All I had were my own anguished recollections of my brother's decline, the jumble of papers from the briefcase and his 'biography' retrieved from the Priory. Recalling those last years of his life from my own memory was painful enough. Piecing together episodes of his chaotic decline by reading Bill's own words written in the enforced sobriety of an addiction clinic – and from the impassive evidence of credit card and bank statements – would prove just as hard.

There were friends and work colleagues who could help, those who knew the 'old' Bill, at least. And there were professionals like Robin Lefever at Promis and Nick Charles at the Chaucer who had tried to treat him. They would surely have had some insight. I approached Bill's ex-wife, Ruth, who found it just too painful to 'go through again', as she told me in a sensitive and affectionate letter. She wished to 'remember the Bill I knew and loved – not the stranger he became'.

Barbara Jones had been intensely involved – but by now she was living out of the country, pursuing a new career as a war correspondent, filing courageous reports from Afghanistan and Iraq, following a path into danger that Bill himself might once have followed. Perhaps she was trying to tell him something. I felt it better perhaps, in spite of Barbara's love for my brother, in spite of her efforts almost to the very end to help save him, to let her have her own say at a time that she might choose.

There were those of course who could tell me much more. For now I chose not to approach the Hanleys – the brother in prison, or the sister wherever she was. For a start I did not have a clue what to ask them – unsure even if I could find the courage to meet them at all. Eventually I would.

'What do you hope to achieve?' an old colleague of Bill's asked me when I first told him I was considering writing a book about my brother. 'Oh, I don't know,' I replied, 'a tribute, I hope. Plus some advice for those who get caught in the middle.' The story of Bill's fall into cocaine and alcohol addiction, I thought, might also be a warning to others. Find out the truth, I thought, tell it straight and let others decide.

I began to write what I knew. It was a tortuous and unpredictable process, unlike any piece of journalism I had ever undertaken before. I was used to writing 3,000 words in a morning for the *Mail*. Now I was lucky if I wrote 300.

Some days I spent simply staring at the computer screen. At other times the whole undertaking seemed impossible and I would have to escape from the house for a few hours before I could even think of trying to recollect anything more. But there were also sudden moments of clarity, a dawning of what Bill himself might have been feeling during his last months alive. I could not give up now. In the end I came to realise that getting Bill's story 'out there' for total strangers to read, instead of festering inside me, would be my release.

Strangers were slowly becoming confidants, the investigators who were guiding me along the dark road of crime and retribution I been so reluctant to go down.

At first they had treated me with suspicion – as if I might myself be part of the conspiracy. Little by little they revealed more – then came the meeting at HM Treasury and the agreement by Anil Gogna, the chief investigator, to let me see the evidence, brought by the prosecution, in the main trial held at Woolwich that had lasted from June 2000 to July 2001. There it was, the results of over three years of undercover investigations, names, dates, places, timings, transcripts of bugged conversations.

It would be simple enough, so I thought, to compare the

investigative facts of a criminal prosecution, however complicated, with what I knew of Bill's slow-motion self-destruction. It was not at all simple. This is what I discovered:

As Bill embarked on his obsessional love affair with Alex Hanley in 1994, her younger brother, Kevin, was transmuting himself from Fulham flower-seller to cocaine quartermaster for a career criminal with aspirations to be the biggest player in Europe. Just how and when remained hidden. Customs would not tell me – and it had not emerged in any press reports thus far. Everything pointed to Brian Wright as the ruthless wheeler-dealer who somehow made contact with suppliers from South America and took his protégé Kevin into the conspiracy. The deal, whoever made it, was simple enough; half of the wholesale proceeds to the suppliers, half to the 'Organisation' – who would wholesale the drugs in Britain, Europe and Australia. The cocaine itself was supplied on credit – although large amounts of cash would have had to be laid out first on the means to get it across the Atlantic.

The cocaine would arrive by boat. The seafaring expertise would have to come from the Caribbean end while the South American suppliers would also involve their own representatives. Hence the bizarre cast of characters who would eventually end up in the dock at Woolwich – Fulham cabbies, an ex-jockey, a Brazilian 'economist', and a rogues' gallery of grizzled American seafarers.

One of these seafarers was a middle-aged US citizen named James Goodrich – 'a salty sea dog', as Customs described him to me – who had been in and out of the Caribbean drug business for years. He owned a yacht, the *Casita*, capable of crossing the Atlantic, and in early 1996 he was looking for gainful employment. Goodrich had multiple aliases. His nickname was 'Popeye'. In 1996 he was calling himself 'Alan Paxton'.

The full story of what the Organisation had been up to thereafter would only come tumbling out four years later when James Goodrich did a plea-bargain in a Miami courtroom, and US Drug Enforcement Authority agents informed their British counterparts that their suspect might have useful information.

Interviewed by British Customs officers, he revealed details of the Wright Organisation's first alleged cocaine-running mission evidently made in July 1996.

Goodrich, looking for work, had first made contact with a group of suppliers in Venezuela, through a man known as 'Mad Dog', who had a forty-two-year-old American girlfriend called Judith Parks. Goodrich was told to fly to the Hilton Hotel in Caracas to receive instructions. In the Venezuelan capital he met a man he called 'Rock Star', whom he described in his later evidence as 'a representative of the Colombian cartel'. Also present at the meeting was a man called 'Kiko', known, because of a florid skin complaint, as 'Pinky' – and some kind of assistant called 'Flaco'.

According to his evidence, the Colombians told Goodrich to find both a suitably discreet harbour for the drugs to be loaded in Venezuela and go to Britain to find a site for their landing – where the cartel's eager new customer, the Wright Organisation, would be waiting. 'Flaco' would go too just to make sure. Putting the reception operation together was someone I had met for Christmas drinks at Bill's house eighteen months before. It was Kevin Hanley.

James Goodrich, alias Alan Paxton, duly came to London in April 1996 with instructions to stay at the Forum Hotel on the Cromwell Road, Kensington, one of the Wright Organisation's favoured meeting places. He soon set off on a reconnaissance of the south coast, settling on the Poole area in Dorset as being the best location for the English end of the delivery. Goodrich then returned to Venezuela.

The Organisation had the boats for two planned Atlantic runs. They now needed innocent-looking yachts to make the transfer at sea and the means to bring it ashore undetected – the old smugglers' trick known as 'coopering'. They also clearly needed some sea-going expertise at the English end. In June 1996 a man named Godfried Hoppenbrouwers, a fifty-five-year-old Dutchman, resident in Brazil, turned up in the Poole area. He was a veteran yachtsman, who had arrived from Holland via ferry in a little Daihatsu 4x4. When Customs at Harwich found satellite navigation equipment and coastal charts of Devon and Cornwall in the vehicle, he told them he was going on a 'fishing trip'.

Someone else was busy in the glittering marinas of Hampshire that summer so the prosecution would allege – Kevin Hanley – squiring the various visitors round the south coast on their 'reconnaissance' operations. It was Hanley, for example, who bought one of them a return ticket to Caracas. Questioned later, staff at the Poole travel agency recalled his apparent attempt to dodge the store security camera and the fact that he paid the fare in cash from a large roll of £50 notes.

The Organisation still needed a boat to meet the first transatlantic visitor and 'cooper' the drugs in the open sea. A boatyard in Poole had a 30-foot yacht called the *Selina*, which looked ideal. The plausible Hoppenbrouwers did the negotiations in person on behalf of the purchaser – named as a 'Mr Anthony Russell' of Chelsea. The weatherbeaten Dutchman gave a mobile phone contact for 'Mr Russell' – 0468 764136. That phone was later identified as the same one allegedly supplied by the Marbella-based businessman, to whoever it was who would prove so anxious to contact the *Sea Mist* when it was under police escort in Cork harbour.

The *Selina* was purchased with a banker's draft, drawn on the account of a finance company, one of the Marbella businessman's ventures. A copy of the draft was faxed on 25 June 1996 to the yachtbrokers on the note paper of the Conrad Hotel in Chelsea Harbour.

On the other side of the Atlantic, meanwhile, Goodrich was ready to take delivery of the drugs from 'Pinky'. According to his testimony, 600 kilos of cocaine were transferred to his care at a derelict hotel on Margarita, an island off the Venezuelan coast. The *Casita* sailed – crewed by Goodrich and another man. They staged at St Maarten in the Dutch Antilles – to begin the transatlantic leg of the drug-delivery run in early June 1996.

Five weeks later the *Casita* was off the coast of Brittany, close enough inshore for a mobile phone to pick up a call. According to his evidence, Goodrich contacted Judith Parks, herself an experienced sailor, who was now in England. She instructed him to go to a point already predetermined in Studland Bay just outside Poole harbour. The *Casita* then set course for the English coast. In the early hours of 18 July, she was 80 miles off Poole.

The *Selina* was also on the move. In fact she left her Poole mooring, the marina records showed, on 4 July 1996, and went to a boatyard across the harbour where some repairs were carried out and a new outboard motor for her inflatable dinghy procured. The bills were paid by 'Mr Russell', who had written his details on the order forms. They would later be shown to be in the handwriting of Kevin Hanley.

On the night of 15–16 July, the *Selina* set off for the rendezvous. Hanley and Judith Parks were aboard. The *Casita* met the *Selina* with little ceremony. The drugs were transshipped in little more than five minutes. The *Casita*'s captain, according to his testimony, was handed a first payment of £5,500 in cash.

Where the *Selina* made landfall, investigators could not discover. But they were convinced that the cargo had been deftly loaded into waiting vans to be spirited into Hanley's distribution chain.

The now drugless *Casita* could make harbour safely, its two-man crew grateful enough for a break ashore after five weeks at sea. On 19 July she entered Lymington harbour. There was a celebration dinner that night at the Stanwell House Hotel in the seaside town's pretty high street, with Goodrich, 'Pappy' Hoppenbrouwers, Kevin Hanley, Judith Parks and 'Flaco' all toasting their success amid the respectable fellow diners.

The team had a further dinner at a pub run by a lady called 'Gloria' who was known to Kevin. One of the people working at the pub was another girlfriend of Hanley's called Anni Rowland.

James Goodrich wanted the rest of his money. He received a series of payments totalling $750,000 in London, usually made over at the Holiday Inn on the Cromwell Road by Flaco, he testified. The money was in cash, in sterling, and in bundles with a note folded over each block of money. The largest single payment was £100,000.

A second boat was coming – the *Sea Mist*. Members of the

Wright Organisation, including Kevin Hanley and Brian Brendon's thirty-year-old son, also named Brian Wright, were later tracked by investigators to having been in key locations in Venezuela and the Caribbean in early August 1996, as the second skipper, Gordon Richards, made ready to sail. It all went wrong in Cork harbour, but the drama had not ended there.

A renewed 'coopering' operation had been set up to meet the *Sea Mist*. This time the *Casita*, drug-boat number one – and for the past two months the respectable resident of Lymington harbour – would make the transfer at sea. James Goodrich had been persuaded to reluctantly skipper the coopering mission – insisting meanwhile that the *Sea Mist*, a converted deep-ocean trawler, was going to excite suspicion if it came anywhere near land.

The *Sea Mist*, of course, never arrived. The Motorola phone on the trawler's bridge had gone off as it was on its way to being impounded in Cork harbour with Irish police aboard. In this reply, Roman Smolen had indicated what was happening to whoever it was on the '136' phone at the other end. James Goodrich also took a call from someone on the same '136' phone while going round in circles in the Solent aboard the *Casita* waiting for the *Sea Mist* to make its rendezvous: 'The boat's gone down – get out!' he was told.

30

I can only guess how much Bill knew about these first missions. I suspect nothing, so tight was the Organisation's 'security' – until the *Sea Mist* fiasco, and that was an accident of the weather. But Bill was by now surely aware that Kevin Hanley was something more than a flower-seller. All I know is that in the summer of 1996 Bill and his girlfriend seemed to be living in some footballers' wives' fantasy – lavish holidays, night-long dinner parties, champagne, and whatever else.

Then in the autumn there was all that stuff about baseball bats and 'a gun in the garden'. Kevin Hanley, as I knew already, had evidently gone to ground in Wiseton Road, the curtains always drawn, the door barred to me and my family even when in search of a working bathroom. I had assumed at the time it was all gangster fiction fantasy. Bill was behaving appallingly meanwhile – rowing with me, rowing with Alex – constantly fired up by some restless anger.

Now Bill's mood and the bizarre events of the second half of that year began to make sense – barrel-chested Barry hovering round Wiseton Road, the revolver in the flowerbed and the carrier bag of money that Bill had himself told me about at the time. These things, and the holdall stuffed with packets of cocaine that Danny McGrory shudderingly described to me as having seen in Bill's kitchen. Why any of these things should have been under my brother's roof, even for a few hours, was beyond my comprehension.

In spite of the *Sea Mist* 'going down', the Organisation was awash with cash that autumn, but none of it seemed to be coming

Bill's way. He told me at the time he was desperate about money. Where was it going?

There were so few clues left. One of them was the document he signed, the one in the briefcase the Customs took in their raid on my house, the lease on the caravan the investigators had been so interested in. I looked at it again – a hire-purchase agreement from the 'Bourne Leisure Group' for a 'used Atlas Fanfare Super', whatever that was. At the top left-hand corner is printed my brother's name and home address. In the top right-hand corner is a box giving his employer: 'The Times, 1 Pennington Street, London'. At the bottom of the agreement are two names. One is Bill's. The other is a 'Mr S. Jennings', supposedly also a resident of his house, No. 6 Wiseton Road, Wandsworth SW17.

The finance deal was evidently struck at Pagham holiday village itself, and some sort of manager acted as witness to Bill's signature. He signed up to pay £21,531 over the next seven years in monthly instalments. The document was dated 17 April 1997.

What was he doing? Two of Bill's friends at *The Times* told me that Bill had confided to them on separate occasions that Kevin Hanley had asked him to buy property in the 'West End'. God knows if he did or not, but why did he tell them?

He never told me. Perhaps it was saloon-bar boasting – perhaps he was looking to get some sense of protection by sharing this surely secret information with his colleagues. 'Hanley and Bill were all very matey at first – then Bill suddenly seemed to become frightened of Kevin,' Danny McGrory would later chillingly tell me.

All I remember of that time was Bill retreating ever further into a shadow world of drawn curtains and half-spoken intimations of something going on that his sister most certainly should not know. He became secretive, distanced, wary of any confidence given on the telephone.

Perhaps, perhaps, I hate to think it, Bill had a reason. As I discovered much later, alerted to the Wright connection by the phone-log evidence from the *Sea Mist*, HM Customs had by now, in the spring of 1997, begun their bugging operation at Chelsea Harbour and fingered Kevin as the Milkman's 'trusted lieutenant'. That the Organisation was now under surveillance must have been obvious. Nevertheless, preparations for the drug-running operations planned for the summer were about to up a gear.

A new character was about to enter the plot – a middle-aged, balding self-styled 'economist', a Brazilian national named Ronaldo Soares. He would be described later by the prosecution as the 'senior and trusted representative of the South American drug suppliers'.

Hotel records found later placed Mr Soares in Trinidad in late May and early June 1997. Others were sent from Britain at the same time, so the prosecution would allege, to organise and provide the finance for the next wave of transatlantic import-ation. A month later Brian Brendon Wright was back in London hosting meetings with Hanley at the Conrad Hotel customs would allege to finalise plans for the cocaine's reception and sale.

In the first two weeks of August 1997, two more yachtsmen, a South African named Gary Boshoff and a sometime journalist called Paul Rodgers, sailed a boat called the *Moonstreak* from Barbados straight to Britain. If there was any attempt to meet it at sea, Customs never discovered it. The yacht, now moored innocently enough among the floating pleasure palaces in Lymington harbour, had arrived with over 300 kilos of cocaine aboard, so Customs would later claim. They supposed that it had simply been discreetly unloaded at the quayside.

A few days later the drugs from the *Moonstreak* went into Hanley's wholesale distribution chain to be sold. The profits were huge. The UK cocaine market was insatiable. The *Sea Mist* losses could be written off. A mountain of money was sloshing around.

The Organisation meanwhile planned a new wave of importation on an even bigger scale. Through the spring of 1998, Customs observed a flurry of meetings at the Conrad between Wright, his son Brian and Kevin Hanley – who was now allegedly joined at these gatherings by his wife, Lena. There was another woman at these meetings, Wright evidently had a girlfriend. Investigators clandestinely observed Kevin and Brian Wright together at South Kensington tube station on 12 May – each making repeated calls from public telephones. Phone records traced the outgoing calls to individual numbers in Colombia and Brazil. Wright then departed for Spain.

In early May, Soares arrived back in London and booked into the Forum Hotel on the Cromwell Road. Phone logs revealed calls from his room to Hanley and other members of the Organisation. This was a rare example of sloppy security – henceforth communications were made by multiple use of public phones and a secure call service using untraceable pre-paid phone cards.

The attention of Customs investigators switched meanwhile to the caravan at Pagham in West Sussex, the seaside trailer park from where Bill would phone me saying that life with the Hanley family was 'doing his head in'.

It was kept under surveillance throughout that summer of 1998.

Customs described it to me as 'South London-on-Sea – full of taxi drivers – that sort of thing, very close-knit', and clearly difficult to observe undetected. 'We knew something was going on but didn't know what,' they admitted. An investigator described a stake-out on a sultry summer night watching Kevin and Lena Hanley disport inside – while a cocaine landing was in fact going on 50 miles away at the other end of the Solent.

Bill was there with Alex that summer, I myself knew that directly. But so far as Customs told me, they had never logged his presence at Pagham nor had any reason to want to do so.

Godfried Hoppenbrouwer's little Daihatsu 4x4 was observed at the 'holiday village', and so were two alleged London-based Organisation members – Barry Fennell, the medallion-man who I had met outside Bill's house, and a taxi driver called Michael O'Connor. Both men were Fulham neighbours of Hanley, and Fennell was suspected of being a key operative in the movement of the drugs once they had been landed. But other than try to track the movements of members of the Organisation, Customs were powerless to find the actual yachts and their cargoes.

What actually happened that summer of 1998 was only put together much later by investigators after painstaking trawls through yachtbrokers' records and the testimony of those like

Alan Goodrich and Judith Parks who would give evidence for the prosecution from jail-cells in America. This time, four yachts were preparing to leave various points in the Caribbean, with crews put together by Soares and Hoppenbrouwers. Roman Smolen was back at the helm of one of them, a boat called the *Lucky Irish*.

The respectable-seeming yachtsman Paul Rodgers was back on the *Moonstreak* (which this time for some reason would only get as far as the Atlantic island of Madeira). A third boat, the *Cyan*, was skippered by Timothy Parks, Judith Parks's brother. The fourth boat, the *Flex*, was skippered by a Frenchman called Claude Rotil. The flotilla sailed between 20 and 30 July, bearing over one and a half tonnes of cocaine.

Their reception was meanwhile being put together. A 46-foot sailing yacht called the *Ramarch* was chartered from 'Sea Ventures' of Lymington Yacht Haven by Hoppenbrouwers and a man with a South African accent calling himself 'H. Johns'. Mr Johns would later be identified as a resident of Savannah, Georgia, named Hilton van Staden.

Operating from Parkstone Yacht Club, prosecutors later alleged that van Staden and his fellow crew member Judith Parks (who had flown in from the Caribbean to do a repeat performance of her coopering endeavours of 1996) used the *Ramarch* to meet at least two of the visitors from the Caribbean in the open sea sometime between 26 and 31 August 1998.

Cocaine was pouring in that late summer – at least 1.2 tonnes of it got through in three boatloads, even after the *Moonstreak* went off on its own curious voyage to Madeira. Who was receiving it? Where was it going? In her own later trial, Judith Parks indicated just who was in control: 'The cocaine was taken to a safe house for storage, packed into boxes and taken away by Hanley,' she stated in a Miami courtroom in late summer 2000. For this work, 'van Staden paid me £35,000 and Hanley £15,000'. Judith Parks also revealed that Kevin had a partner in the cocaine removal business – not a Fulham cabbie but the driver of an expensive four-wheel drive. It was the mother of his infant child, Anni Rowland. 'She boxed it up and loaded it in her car and drove it to a secret location in London', according to Parks's evidence. Brian Wright was back in town meanwhile. On 21 August undercover investigators saw him and Kevin once again in multiple phone-box action, this time in Chiswick. The numbers called were in Spain. That afternoon Kevin was spotted using a phone box in the Pimlico Road, this time in the company of Barry Fennell.

I looked at what I knew of Bill's behaviour in this period. The urgent sale of Wiseton Road, the move to the country with Alex, his appalling behaviour around her, passing out in front of his own celebratory birthday dinner the very week in early September 1998 when, as I now knew, three boatloads of cocaine were being processed somewhere on the south coast by Kevin Hanley to be fed into his distribution chain or moved to some hiding place. More than that, his inbuilt code of self-preservation seemed to be unravelling. I found this in his Priory confessional:

'Before 1998 I had never driven under the influence of either drink or drugs. Now having gone to the pub after work one evening, as well as taken a couple of lines in the lavatory, I thought, "Why not?"

'I went to the multi-storey, got the car and drove home to Oxfordshire. For a brief instant I thought: "This is wrong. Suppose I kill someone?"

'The next thought was, "Fuck it". I carried on like this until I resigned.'

Bill may have known nothing about the drugs fanning out from the New Forest, but his own addictions were rotting his mind and body in front of me. When I begged my brother to tell me what he might have 'done' for Alex's brother, he would just fill a glass, sniff, and stare blankly out of my kitchen window.

But he did do something that year, and he certainly never told me about it. When Customs investigators gave me the details, I was astonished. Sometime in early 1998 Kevin Hanley moved Lena and the family to a new address, 18 Bishops Road in Fulham, a modest if smart Victorian terrace near the North End Road market. Customs kept the house under observation. Discreet inquiries were made at the letting agency in Parsons Green. The rent was £1,500 per month – apparently being paid along with a further £500 of utility bills by someone previously unknown to Customs. The name on the rental agreement was William Robert Frost.

Kevin was making his own financial arrangements that summer. They seemed to be somewhat independent of the Wright Organisation. The facts would only emerge years later – but in the summer of 1998 according to customs investigators, he employed both Anni Rowland and a strange seventy-year-old resident of Notting Hill called Brian Coldwell to move money around. Throughout that summer Anni flew to Geneva several times while Coldwell nursed hidden packets of cash on different Swiss-bound flights. Once in the financial capital, Anni lodged the cocaine millions in discreet accounts, so customs would allege at her eventual trial. Coldwell meanwhile had flown to Sweden on Hanley's account to pay the syndicate who owned the *Flex*, the fourth yacht in that summer's flotilla that had sailed from Chaguaramas in Trinidad (the place where the Sea Mist had been loaded) on 20 July. At his eventual trial Coldwell would testify that the purchase money for the yacht was handed over to him by an anonymous man in a London pub called the Ladbroke Arms.

That summer, Brian Wright's horse-racing activities were exciting the attention of a different branch of law enforcement. In October the previous year, the Jockey Club head of security had urged the Metropolitan Police Organised Crime Group to investigate alleged race-fixing. The following January, three jockeys and four high-rolling punters were arrested – all of whom denied the charges.

On 9 June 1998, police raided Wright's apartment in Chelsea Harbour. The target was missing – Wright was in Spain, but the Milkman returned to London in mid-September to face his accusers in the company of a solicitor at Charing Cross police station. Wright was arrested without charge and bailed to appear again in three months' time. Customs investigators admitted to me that the Metropolitan Police's heavy-handed intervention, clodhopping round the Conrad Hotel, for example, threatened to jeopardise their own much more sensitive snooping into the Organisation's drug operations.

Wright's Chelsea Harbour flat had been searched meanwhile. Police found a 'racing diary' with all kinds of cryptic entries. Examined much later by Customs, it was found to contain contact numbers for the Marbella-based businessman and the mobiles used by Goodrich on the *Casita* mission. They also found an inconsequential looking scrap of newspaper dated two years earlier – the property section of a local newspaper with ads for lets on the Hampshire coast. One was marked up especially – 'Salterns' – a house in Lymington. A mysterious couple had rented it in 1996.

In early October 1998, Ronaldo Soares turned up in London again. So did the South African Gary Boshoff, skipper of the first *Moonstreak* mission, and two other veterans of the preceding two summers' drug-running campaigns – including Paul Rodgers. They met at the Forum Hotel on the Cromwell Road, so prosecutors alleged later, to do their end-of-season accounting and get paid. Large sums of cash were involved. Meetings were held in Boshoff's room, no. 201. It was bugged.

Kevin Hanley was at these sessions. The bugged meetings spoke of huge quantities of cocaine and huge amounts of money – of drug-running missions past and missions yet to come.

Hanley, Customs would tell me, was in effortless command. While he 'was the life and soul of the party – liked a joke, liked his beer, liked Chelsea' – he remained cool and self-controlled. If he took cocaine himself, he was 'a party-user'. Nor was he violent.

Soares was clearly impressed. He said, according to a tape transcript produced at the trial: 'Kevin should be [inaudible], also his organisations here are very good.' All seemed set for another season of mass importation and huge profits.

31

In mid-September 1998 as Customs continued their watch on the Organisation, Bill went to South Africa on a story for *The Times*. Having conducted his interviews, he indulged in a monster drink and cocaine bender, as I discovered later when I read his Priory confessional. On his return from Johannesburg, he looked ruined. I sensed I was losing him – that he was slipping from my grasp, about to go over the edge into what horror I could scarcely imagine. While once Bill would have confided his slightest passing emotion to me, now communication was minimal. When he did talk, none of it made any sense. He was eaten up by a brooding restless anger – suspicious to the point of paranoia.

I knew it was time to act, to get proper professional help, and did what I could to get Bill into Promis, the addiction clinic in Kent from where he discharged himself after only eight days. He returned to Wapping; better, he assured me, to get back to the 'grindstone' of journalism than, I had to assume at the time, be told anything he did was wrong by dictatorial therapists.

But Bill by now inhabited a parallel universe beyond my own or any of his colleagues' understanding. Something was about to happen in the mirror-world from which there could be no escape.

In the early evening of 28 November, Customs got a call from Marylebone police station CID. A driver had been stopped and arrested in Sussex Gardens, near Paddington station in west London, after a 'tip-off'. A black holdall full of packets of white powder had been found in the boot of his car. His name, he said, was Kevin Hanley. Do you know him? asked the police. 'We do,' said Customs, 'we've been after him for two years.'

That awful night when Bill had come hammering at my door out of his head with drugs and raw fear was explained. Of course Bill was terrified – of what he had done, of what was going to happen next. When Christy marched him out the front door, he had gone off raving and ranting to the Conrad Hotel in Chelsea Harbour – to see who or do what I had no idea.

Customs asked for and got a judicial gagging order on any press mention of Kevin's arrest. 'We thought at the time it was a major setback,' an investigator told me.

'For the Organisation?' I asked.

'No, for us,' he replied. 'Hanley was our prime surveillance target – although we knew Wright was behind it all – but he never went hands on. We were anxious that everyone might now run for cover.

'Hanley's arrest meant Wright's right arm was cut off,' he continued. 'We suspected that most of the cocaine shipped earlier in 1998 had neither been paid for yet – nor been sold on. Other than the stuff found in Hanley's car, we did not know where the rest of it was. Wright would most likely shut up shop or try and hand the cocaine back to the suppliers in Colombia. We'd lose it.'

As well as 29 kilos of cocaine and £5,000 in cash, police found a cream 'puffa' jacket in Hanley's secondhand Rover, bought under a false name three weeks earlier. In an inside pocket was a telephone-address-book written up in his distinctive spidery handwriting. Many of the entries were in code.

The Fulham house, the one Bill was paying for, was raided in the early hours of the 29th. Investigators found £13,250 in cash. Lena Hanley was absent.

If Bill's decline into addiction thus far had been grimly measured step-by-step, now he began falling like a stone. It was as if Kevin Hanley's arrest had pushed him off some precipice – there could be no going back, no hope of redemption. All that was left was Alex. He clung to her like a drowning man.

That Christmas and New Year of 1998–9 Bill was beyond

reason. Intoxication was by now permanent. His house was gone, and his last hold on reality, his job, was hanging by a thread. He was out of it – his world shrunken to whatever sofa he could find to slump on and a pair of stereo headphones.

Meanwhile, the main act in the wider drama was about to be played. Just as Customs had feared, after Kevin's arrest Brian Brendon Wright was indeed shutting down. Without his trusted lieutenant, The Milkman could not shift the cocaine. Without shifting the cocaine, paying the suppliers was problematic (even if Wright was estimated to be worth £100 million in a BBC 'underworld rich list' compiled in 2004). Wright had heart trouble. Earlier that month he had had major cardiac surgery in the private Wellington Hospital in St John's Wood. The crisis had come.

Ronaldo Soares flew urgently back from Brazil to sort it out, arriving in London around 11 December. This time he stayed at the La Gaffe Hotel, a relatively modest establishment set above an Italian restaurant in Hampstead, north London. He booked in as 'Mr Ronaldo' and pre-paid a week's bill in cash.

Soares was tailed. He was observed in Highgate, north London. A bill for the purchase of a mobile phone was retrieved from a litter bin. On 15 December the South American emissary was observed meeting the convalescent Wright at Sloane Square tube station – from where they went to a pub in Pimlico. There were several more meetings in the period before Wright disappeared to Spain.

It was all a bit of a cock-up. Customs were clearly surprised to see Wright show up in person. An undercover officer posing as a telecom engineer got a photograph of Soares but not Wright (code named 'Target Z-7'). A female investigator had the same experience hiding in a florist's shop opposite a Pimlico Pub – the Orange Tree Brewery – where both men had gone. But the fact that Wright, the untouchable Uncle, had broken cover at all was very significant.

This is what Customs believed happened. Wright would not pay up. He urged Soares to take back the cocaine that Hanley had not already sold before his arrest – more than half a tonne of it. Soares said no, we want our money. Wright stood firm. The Brazilian at last reluctantly agreed: he would find his own way of getting rid of it if Wright's remaining 'gofers' – the ones that Hanley had controlled – provided transport. Around christmas eve, believing he was clear of the damage, Wright flew to Spain.

On 7 February Soares plus Barry Fennell were seen in the company of a twenty-three-year-old woman in the Café Rouge restaurant near Hampstead tube station in north London. She was identified as a Ms Liliana Uribe, a 'student' from Bogota in Colombia. A bulky holdall was observed being placed in the boot of her silver Peugeot.

Money was clearly being offloaded. There was still the unsold cocaine from the summer 1998 importations stored wherever Hanley had hidden it. Ronaldo Soares indeed did seem to have his own contact, someone who was not part of the Wright Organisation. He was called Roger Douglas Newton, a forty-year-old 'carpenter' and suburban family man who had played a shadowy part in the Caribbean in 1997, preparing the first *Moonstreak* mission. Ronaldo Soares had called him regularly during his 1998 stay in London. He was listed in Hanley's phone book as 'Ron's friend'.

In late January 1999, Soares was followed by Customs investigators to Newton's address, 81 The Ridgeway, a semi-detached house in the sleepy Essex village of Chalkwell near Westcliff-on-Sea. The Brazilian stayed overnight. More meetings followed.

Barry Fennell was back on the move. He was observed on 8–9 February making multiple phone calls from public phone boxes in Fulham where he lived – and also in Wandsworth and Tooting near Bill's old house in Wiseton Road and indeed my own. Phone company records showed he called Soares's mobile and a number in Holland. That evening he took delivery of a hired white Transit van which he drove to Hampstead to be inspected late that night by Soares, presumably for its suitability as a drugs transporter.

On 10 February one of the gang was allegedly observed in the company of a man named Paul Shannon, an associate of Kevin's, already identified by investigators as Brian Brendon Wright's former son-in-law. Around lunchtime that same day, Ronaldo Soares met Roger Newton at Paddington station. Early in the afternoon they went, after a complicated shuffle on the Underground, via Waterloo mainline to Staines station near Heathrow. They waited in a café. Barry Fennell was soon observed arriving in a yellow pick-up truck. Soares went back to north London, but Newton and Fennell drove to a scrubby suburban 'farm' at Ashford Road, Laleham, Middlesex – a jumble of industrial units, one of which was rented to a firm called 'Car and Commercial Services'.

The white Transit hired by Fennell, shown off to Soares late the night before, had evidently been parked there earlier that morning. It was observed emerging with Roger Newton behind the wheel followed by Fennell in his yellow pick-up. The little convoy soon split up. The 'D & D Van Hire' Transit was followed clockwise round the M25, heading apparently for Newton's home at Chalkwell. Instead the van stopped outside a lock-up garage behind an anonymous-looking block of flats grandly named 'Hampton Court' in Lymington Avenue, Leigh-on-Sea, a few miles to the west. It was rented by Newton's father.

The next day, 11 February, Soares was watched buying thirteen sports-bags at a shop in Oxford Street. He then went by train to Leigh-on-Sea to hand them over (he left his fingerprints on one of them). He was clearly in a hurry. One of the gang meanwhile was observed making multiple calls from a public phone box in Fulham. It was time for Customs to move.

The Customs 'knock' came down in a synchronised rap early on the morning of Friday 12 February 1999. Over 150 police and Customs national investigation service officers raided addresses across London and southern England.

At 6.35 a.m., the Bishops Road house, the one Bill was apparently paying for, was raided for the second time. A number of mobile phones were seized and a torn-out piece of Filofax paper found with telephone numbers in Holland and Belgium (the same numbers were soon to be found in the possession of

Soares and Fennell). This time Lena Hanley was arrested – and charged with conspiracy to supply cocaine.

At 7.08 a.m., Newton was roused from his Essex bed. The 'Hampton Court' lock-up was opened with a key he blinkingly provided. Some 550 kilograms of cocaine were found inside; some of the 1-kilo packets were still in the cardboard boxes they had arrived in, and some had been stuffed in the sports-bags Soares had delivered the afternoon before.

When interviewed, Newton said he thought the boxes contained pornography. 'He was frightened and scared for his family and young children . . . He said that he was terrified. There was no point in talking to him because he had nothing further to add.'

'Residents were shocked by the raid which has rocked their quiet community and were surprised to hear of Mr Newton's arrest,' so a local newspaper reported quaintly a few days later before a total news blackout was imposed.

At 7.13 a.m., 30 miles to the west of the Essex lock-up, 'Mr Ronaldo' was arrested in Room 17 of La Gaffe Hotel in Hampstead. He 'gradually revealed a series of substantial amounts [of cash] in various places,' according to the trial evidence.

Brian Wright junior got the pre-dawn knock at his house in Weybridge, Surrey. Barry Fennell was picked up at the Inglenook Hotel, Pagham, not far from the caravan. When his house at 9 Breer Street in Fulham was searched, a witness statement from one of the police officers involved with Kevin's arrest was found. The taxi driver Mick O'Connor was arrested at his nearby flat in Peterborough Road, and letters to him sent by Hanley when in custody were discovered. They were later used for forensic comparison of Kevin's handwriting – including the purchase documents for the *Selina*'s outboard motor.

The Marbella-based financier was also arrested. Two other men, Ian Kiernan and Paul Shannon, both long-time members of the Organisation, were also arrested at their homes. Customs described them to me as 'gofers'. Within the Organisation they were known, along with Brian Junior, as 'the boys'.

Officers went to Liliana Uribe's flat in Earls Court later that morning. In a number of bags they found a total of £90,000 and $127,454 in cash. She was arrested.

The Laleham farm was searched that afternoon. Another 29 kilos of cocaine were found in a second white van hired two months earlier by Barry Fennell. The total weight of drugs from both seizures was 472.77 kilos broken down into 464 packets. The wholesale value was estimated at £14 million, the street value at £59 million.

The suspects were taken to Lyndhurst police station in Hampshire in the middle of the New Forest, interviewed and charged. The place sounded like some rural lock-up. When I went much later to have a look at it myself, it was like a high-security military base.

That evening, BBC online news posted a short bulletin: 'Thirteen people have been arrested after half a tonne of cocaine was seized. The Customs National Investigation Service says the haul is their biggest seizure of the drug for years and that it believes a major international drugs ring has been disrupted.

'Officers said the operation had seriously disrupted a major trafficking organisation responsible for smuggling cocaine from South America to the rest of the world.

'The raids followed a two-year surveillance operation, which saw investigators follow the cocaine to the lock-up after it was brought into Britain by boat.

' "It's one of the largest seizures in the last two or three years. It will have a significant impact upon the availability of cocaine in the UK," said a spokesman . . .' Any further newspaper coverage remained minimal, and Kevin and Lena Hanley were never mentioned. A full news blackout was ordered very soon afterwards on any further reporting whatsoever.

The race-fixing allegations against 'Uncle' Brian had been dropped meanwhile on the advice of the Crown Prosecution Service. Brian Wright seemed to have vanished. The Dutch-Brazilian sailor 'Pappy' Hoppenbrouwers and the South African Gary Boshoff had also disappeared. International arrest warrants were issued on 24 February 1999 for those allegedly in the conspiracy who had evaded the net. But when Spanish police called at El Lechero, the Milkman himself had flown.

It was Kevin Hanley's arrest that had brought Ronaldo Soares back to London and sent Brian Wright scurrying off to Spain. It was Kevin's arrest that seemed to plunge Bill into his pit of terrified despair. It was the turning moment of the story, perhaps of my brother's life. It was the result of an 'anonymous tip-off'. By who?

It was clearly a matter of the utmost sensitivity even after almost seven years. At our Treasury meeting in January 2005, Customs officials were very reluctant to tell me. Mike Torpy had mentioned somewhere along the line that it had been 'a bent policeman' who had been the informer. I tried that line on my hosts.

'OK,' said Anil Gogna. 'We'll tell you. Actually he had at one time been a Met Police cadet – that's all. His name is Graham Piper.'

The mysterious Mr Piper seems to have been a junior version of the Milkman – a gambler and racehorse owner who allegedly dabbled in the coke business. He was himself arrested in February 1999 following a Metropolitan Police anti-drugs operation not linked to Operation Extend. Why did Piper do it? 'We don't know exactly,' Customs told me, 'but we believe it was a deal with Hanley that went wrong and Piper could not pay for the cocaine so he returned it.' Piper was found guilty at the Old Bailey and sentenced to fourteen years in 2001 – but a reporting ban as other trials progressed kept the whole matter secret for almost three years afterwards.

Soon after Piper's arrest, Customs officers went to see Kevin Hanley in Wandsworth prison and, with the evidence from yacht-charter and phone records, 'arrested' him again on the further charge of 'being knowingly concerned in the importation of a controlled drug'. Thus far, 'possession with intent to supply' of the drugs found in the car had been a police case. Charged with importation, Kevin was now facing a sentence of thirty years. He admitted nothing.

The Milkman might have vanished, but his Organisation had

been taken to pieces. Bill's world had fallen apart in parallel. His behaviour in those first weeks and months of 1999 – sleeping in his car, bragging about 'crack' to his colleagues, taking maniacal drug-taking risks in the office – became somehow understandable. Perhaps he half wanted to be found out – for the anguish to end.

Virtually everything about the 12 February wave of arrests, I reminded myself, was secret at the time. Then, on 1 March 1999, the *Racing Post* published its embargo-breaking story about the warrant for the disappeared Wright following the seizure two weeks before of '440 kg of cocaine from a garage at Leigh-on-Sea, on the Essex coast . . . which led to 13 arrests in eight different locations in the South East of England. Further arrests are expected.' I think Bill must have seen that. I think that must have frightened him witless.

At no point was Bill under direct surveillance, so Customs investigators stressed to me. At no point was he considered to be party to the cocaine importation conspiracy. As far as they were concerned, William Robert Frost was some sort of 'respectable' front-man with a bank account and salaried employment. Now even that was about to come to an end.

Bill filed his last story for his newspaper on 16 March 1999. It was about a 'radical Muslim cleric, Abu Hamza al-Masri', being 'arrested in a dawn raid and questioned by anti-terrorist squad officers'. The by-line was shared with Danny McGrory. Then Bill quit – to take the severance money and spend it on his doomed trip to Arizona. On the 29th he was on the plane for America. He had returned after three months of star-studded rehab looking miraculously fit, headed for the country with Alex, then embarked pretty much straightaway, I would find out, back on his course of self-destruction.

But in work or not, there was one last thing he might 'do' for the Hanley family. The Customs investigator Anil Gogna told me about it at our meeting at the Treasury. In late July 1999, Lena Hanley was put up for a bail appearance at Woolwich Magistrates Court. Bill was there and so was Anil. He described my brother's appearance in court that day almost six years earlier, shuffling, broken, borne up by Alex.

'Bill Frost came to the bail application,' he told me. 'We knew his name so far only as the person paying the bills at Bishops Road. He gave evidence and offered to stand security – more than £200,000 as I remember.'

'Why was Bill there – where did he get the money?' I asked feebly.

'It seemed straightforward,' said Anil. 'Hanley's got no job, no apparent source of income. He's put up a respectable *Times* reporter to get his wife out of Holloway prison – and let her get back to his kids. Kevin has no bank account – yet he must have had millions.

'Bill was extremely nervous and struggling to stand in the witness box,' Anil continued. 'The hearing had to be stopped three times because he was shaking so much.'

I myself was shaking as the Customs officer dispassionately recalled my brother's condition. He had just come out of rehab – for God's sake. There I was telling him to find a job – telling him everything would be OK now. I bit my lip as I thought of Bill poured into a suit and produced in a courtroom for this gruesome performance. He had never told me a word.

32

Operation Extend was by no means over. The wave of arrests was just the beginning. 'We had bodies and we had cocaine – lots of it,' Customs would tell me. 'Now we had to prove the connections to make our case for court.' The trawl through yachtbrokers' books, the exhaustive search of phone records, the cross-referencing of address books and number-bearing scraps of paper took months of work. Kevin Hanley's coded diary would prove the key.

Investigators had been poring over that diary since soon after the moment it was found in his car. Contact telephone numbers were written in a seemingly simple code – a random sequence of ten-letter nonsense words. A letter's place in the word would result in a number. When decrypted and checked, many of the numbers were in Colombia, Trinidad or Brazil.

The yachts themselves, casually abandoned when the cocaine and cash were flowing, were located one by one and examined forensically. The *Casita*, for example, buccaneeringly 'coopered' by Hanley and Judith Parks in the high-rolling days of the summer of 1996, was discovered three years later in Guernsey. The hiding places for drugs that James Goodrich had built into the yacht were found when he later told the authorities where to look.

The *Cyan*, owned by Hoppenbrouwers and skippered across the Atlantic by Judith Parks's brother in 1998, was discovered abandoned in a boatyard in Cherbourg, France. The yacht had been boarded in December and, according to the dockyard workers, had 'a bad smell' below decks. A package of white powder was found jammed under a locker. The powder was cocaine, marked with the logo 'Chino'.

The cocaine itself found in the Leigh-on-Sea lock-up provided crucial physical evidence. Those packets still in boxes were bulked up with newspaper (the *Mail on Sunday* for 6 September 1998) and pages from local papers from the New Forest area dated around the same time – suggesting to investigators 'the idea that somewhere in that area the Organisation had a safe house where the drugs could be wrapped and boxed before they were taken to London'. Kevin's seafaring partner Judith Parks would later describe a 'purple house' near Ringwood in Hampshire 'next to a stream beside a school'. She estimated two tonnes of cocaine had been moved through it – with Anni Rowland doing much of the shifting. Every cupboard and the loft had been stuffed. The New Forest purple-house was never found by investigators.

The 1-kilo packets themselves were 'branded' by degree of purity and as a stock-keeping method: 'Joker', 'Ace of Spades', 'Uncle Sam', 'Chino', 'NN' and so on. Twenty-two of the packages that came out of the Leigh-on-Sea garage were the 'Chino' brand, the same as that found on the *Cyan* abandoned in Cherbourg. A stock-taking scrawl on one box, listing the contents, was in Kevin Hanley's distinctive handwriting. Hanley's diary found in the car referred to them by the same names, monitoring stock levels and payments.

Only now from the jumble of abandoned yachts and their contents, from the examination of satellite navigation handsets and tidal charts, from the decrypting of Hanley's phone book, were investigators able to put together a picture of what they had missed in the summer of 1998 – when at least four drug-stuffed yachts had criss-crossed the Atlantic to unload their cargoes.

Gordon Richards, the *Sea Mist*'s hapless captain, was re-interviewed in Cork prison. He also provided more useful information, but his testimony was judged to be unreliable in preparing the prosecution case – especially when he turned out not to be Mr Richards of Brighton, England, after all. He was a US citizen called John Earl Ewart.

'Alan Paxton', the *Casita*'s skipper, had been lifted in May 1998 when attempting to smuggle almost 2 tonnes of cocaine into Fort Lauderdale, Florida, on a boat called the *Five Stars*. His real name was at last revealed as James Goodrich.

'We went to see him in prison,' Customs told me. 'He just flipped. The Americans did a plea-bargain and he gave us a lot of information to fill in the jigsaw.' Goodrich's evidence would be at the heart of the UK prosecution case.

In September 1999 the yachtsman Paul Rodgers (described to me by Customs as a 'Walter Mitty character') was arrested at a house outside Portsmouth and his computer seized. It contained a half-completed adventure novel about sea-borne drug-running, references to (real) yacht movements and the name and address of Hilton van Staden. Rodgers admitted being at the crucial planning meetings in London in October 1998, but told his interrogators the name Ronaldo Soares meant nothing to him.

Four months later 'Pappy' Hoppenbrouwers was arrested in Florida on a US warrant. In spite of HM Customs attempts to extradite him, he was charged in Miami with money-laundering and involvement in Goodrich's huge Florida cocaine importation attempt in May 1998.

Roman Smolen and Hilton van Staden were arrested in early 2000, van Staden as he attempted to open a London security deposit box full of cash.

In February 2000 Liliana Uribe stood trial at the Old Bailey. She was reported to have become 'embroiled in an £800 million cocaine smuggling conspiracy having fallen in love with a 45-year-old Colombian millionaire'. Press coverage of the trial was minimal. The Soares–Fennell connection was never mentioned. The judge, Mr Justice Stephen Mitchell, told her that 'she had shown great courage in pleading guilty to money-laundering' and was prepared to be lenient. On the 28th she was sentenced to two and a half years.

33

Whether Bill was aware of or took any notice of the continuing arrests I cannot say. Whether he ever met or even knew the names of the alleged conspirators other than Hanley or Barry Fennell I can only guess. But whether he was frightened the forces of law and order were about to come after him is another matter. It would be, as I would discover, a different branch of HM Customs, asset recovery, that had begun to take an interest in his affairs after discovering who was apparently paying the bills for the Hanley household in Fulham.

Two months after the first wave of arrests in February 1999, Bill was out of it, literally, in the deserts of Arizona. After he returned to England, he passed the rest of that year in a blur, lolling round with Alex in the country and, as I discovered, making his trembling court appearance in July to stand bail in London for Lena Hanley. After that he shut himself away alone in that Notting Hill basement, barely able to move across the room – until Barbara Jones scooped him up and bravely tried to put what was left of him back together.

His urge to work, the passion for journalism, had evaporated entirely. The matter of our cousin's will – leaving the bulk of his fortune to charity and the rest to my children or any that Bill might claim – seemed to have knocked the last vestiges of self-respect out of him. 'I could do with a quarter of a million right now,' he had told me that autumn – not in rueful humour, but in resentful anger.

On the last day of the twentieth century, Bill and I talked warmly enough on the phone of new hope and new prospects. I invited him to come with us to a party being held by old friends in north London who had known Bill for years – the old Bill that is. He said he would rather not. I don't remember where he was that night when the new millennium dawned.

All I know is that in those first weeks and months of 2000 Bill was incapable of comprehending anything of the real world as he was passed like a parcel between whoever still cared. Barbara Jones could not tolerate his behaviour any longer, nor could his old friends the Hearns. Alex Hanley would not have him, nor could I. The stay with our cousin Sheilagh in the country waiting for the prayed-for admission to the Chaucer had ended in disaster. He had broken out to get to London, met and rowed hugely with Barbara in some Soho bar, then got out of his head and piled his car into a tree. I thought it fleetingly at the time, and have considered it since – perhaps he wanted to end it all right there and then.

Then in early March 2000 Bill got perhaps his best chance when the Chaucer, the battered charity hospital in Ealing, at last admitted him. The first weeks were rough certainly, but then he buckled down. He seemed to be getting better. He might get clean, I began to hope, get back to work, and do what he clearly wanted most – get back to Alex.

Bill was coming out of detox as Kevin Hanley's trial was set to begin *in camera* at the Old Bailey on 24 March, with Lena as co-defendant. Still Kevin would not plead guilty. A Customs official told me he asked Kevin directly why he did not just 'admit to the lot'. He was now facing a sentence of over thirty years. 'You don't know what would happen,' Kevin had replied.

Then at the last minute Kevin changed his plea to guilty on both counts – possession and importation with intention to supply. Customs told me: 'He changed his plea after more and more evidence had been served.' The prosecutors decided to drop the charges against Lena.

Kevin's defending counsel described his client as 'a salesman' – a lowly operative in the Wright Organisation. Compared with the other alleged conspirators, Messrs Brian Wright Senior and Ronaldo Soares, he was 'a lieutenant, not a general'. Mr Justice

Mitchell seemed unconvinced. On Kevin's plea of guilty, sentencing was deferred until the end of the main trial due to open at Woolwich in six weeks' time.

While Kevin was facing his accusers at the Old Bailey, Ronaldo Soares was discovered allegedly trying to escape from remand prison, so Customs investigators would tell me. Huge quantities of cash were presumably still at his disposal on the outside to bribe or bust his way out. Other suspects were still at large. That is why the main trial would be held in Woolwich Crown Court, specially convened next to the top-security Belmarsh prison in south-east London.

Just as the trial was about to begin, Barrie Wright, the former jump jockey and an old racecourse confidant of 'Uncle' Brian, was arrested in Belgium and extradited to Britain. He was alleged to have travelled to the Caribbean on behalf of the Milkman in 1996–7.

For legal reasons, it was determined that Smolen, the Marbella-based businessman, Barrie Wright and van Staden would be tried separately in Southampton and Bristol. The main hearing would take fourteen months – the longest Customs trial in English criminal history.

It began in closed session at Woolwich before Mr Justice Mitchell on 2 May 2000, three days before Bill prematurely discharged himself from the Chaucer claiming he had been 'called back to work'. There was no work – there was just me, his sister, who fixed him up with some overlooked money from an insurance policy, and Alex, his on-off girlfriend, who soon after found him the flat in Anselm Road where he might spend it. For a few days, weeks maybe, he struggled to stay clean. Then he gave up.

What was he thinking as he shut himself away in his self-made prison? He would not answer the door or pick up the phone. He was eaten up with fear, drug-induced or otherwise. Going out even to buy food was a 'paranoid nightmare', as he wrote in his Priory confessional. By now he could barely walk. What was he afraid of in the world outside?

This is what I discovered later. The search for Hanley's

presumed millions in hidden drugs' money had begun. Bill's name had already come up as an 'associate' – his name was on the rental agreement for Kevin's house and he had offered the year before to stand bail for his wife. Investigators were beginning to take an interest in Bill's bank account, track his past movements, and try to find his current whereabouts. He had been arrested for drunk driving in February 2000 and given an address, somewhere in Sussex, where he was staying with his cousin, Sheilagh Frost. The address was now on the police computer.

Did Bill know that he was coming under investigation? I suspect he did. Had someone warned him? From what I would be told later by investigators it seems very likely. Was it guilt, was it fear? Was it both of these things? Was that why *he had to get out* of it?

At the time, I knew nothing of the trial proceedings which were now underway in secret at Woolwich. However much Bill might have known, he was in no state to tell me that summer even if he had wanted to as I wheeled him from Casualty department to Casualty department. Then came that last miraculous chink of hope, the concession by *The Times* in August 2000 and their agreement, brokered by Dr Gordon, to fund the admission to the Priory.

The main trial of the alleged cocaine conspirators was in its fifth week when Bill was admitted to the 'celebrity asylum', and in its eleventh week when he was discharged. A degree at least of self-knowledge had been restored. 'I have become a person I don't recognise, a person I don't like,' wrote my brother in his confessional.

'I feel enslaved and hopeless. My bank balance has tumbled as I spend on vodka and cocaine. I've wasted thousands. I have really hurt the people I love most. My sister worries all the time. After losing both parents, she thinks I'll go next – and soon.

'The catalogue of selfishness and stupidity leaves me feeling shame and guilt on a grand scale. Why anyone has stuck by me is baffling.

'But there is hope. I'm here for me and I *must* make this work. It feels like a last chance and probably is.'

* * *

I was certain of it. It was the last chance. Why did Bill not admit it outright himself? I remembered what I could of his last weeks alive.

At his request, it was Alex who came to pick him up from the Priory. She drove him to the flat in Fulham, rearranged the furniture as if to create a new start to his life, then left to see a female friend. Bill was angry. He wanted her to stay, believed it would be different.

Alex needed more time, she had told him, to see if he meant what he said about being 'clean'. Bill felt let down, he said, when I rang with some post-rehab platitudes about everything being all right now. Alex did not 'care', he said; she had left him on his own. Bill hated being alone. He always hated being alone. Her attitude was enough, he had told her, 'to make him use again'.

And that is what he did. 'Coke is everywhere,' he had told me years before, 'it finds you.' There seemed to be no shortage in Fulham.

I took him to a follow-up appointment at the Priory in the first week of October. After that I had to trust him to make it to Roehampton on his own, once a week by minicab. I think he made one, maybe two, appointments. I thought he was being lazy. I did not understand then, but wish I had, that his paranoia was now so overwhelming he could not have stepped outside his own front door without me there to hold his hand.

On a chilly morning in early November, Christy and Joe had a bicycle crash on the way to school. Joe was fine (after the firemen cut him out of the front wheel), but my husband was hobbling about on crutches with a broken pelvis. I was getting used to such things. Life had been a war zone for the past two years after all.

Bill's calls from Anselm Road kept coming, although more fitfully now. There were the usual rants about Alex, but there were other calls full of affection and childish gratitude, with 'I love you' murmured at the end.

I went over a couple of times and did what I could. Loyal, good Danny McGrory turned up on his doorstep and managed to get him out of the flat to go a few hundred yards for a pizza. Lines were going dead. Hardly anyone wanted to know.

I cannot remember the last time I saw Bill alive – only the last time we should have seen one another. A call came early in the morning of Friday, 25 November. I was at my desk at home, about to start work for the day.

Bill's voice sounded agitated and breathless: 'Clare, sorry to bother you. I know I'm a pain . . . But do you know whether Iceland deliver?'

Right on cue, I thought, what now? For a moment I felt supremely irritated. Iceland, the frozen food store, stood on the North End Road just a few yards from the flat. Was Bill really telling me he could not walk that far? Another trip to Casualty seemed to be looming. My irritation turned to acute anxiety.

I put the phone down – and started to worry more. Did he really want me to get some shopping? He never ate anything even when I did. Christy said: 'Don't you dare even think of it. It's just an excuse to get you over there. Don't go. You are exhausted.'

Next Maria rang, and I told her about the call. 'You must go, Mummy,' my daughter said. 'You would never forgive yourself if anything happened. Perhaps he really is hungry and too weak to walk across the road by himself. I'm coming over later. I'll go with you to see him.'

I felt suddenly relieved, knowing this was the right thing to do. I rang Bill to say I was coming. There was no reply.

Maria came over at lunchtime and we drove to Sainsbury's in Fulham together, stocking up on tins of soup and frozen pizza, anything we could think of that Bill might eat. We reached his flat just after two o' clock. Maria ran up the steps and rang the doorbell as I put some money into the parking machine.

'He's not answering,' she called to me from across the street.

'I'm sure he's there,' I replied. 'Perhaps he's asleep. Keep trying.'

We rang the bell, banged on the door and tried our best to peer into the ground floor bay window. The curtains were tightly drawn. There was no response. I felt angry now, having come all this way, bought him food and everything. I wasn't going to give up so easily. I called his number on my mobile. No answer.

Suddenly Maria whispered, 'Mummy, look, the curtain.' I turned just in time to catch the smallest twitch, as if someone were standing behind the curtain watching us, waiting for us to give up and go home. I banged harder. 'Bill, it's me . . . Maria's here with me.' I didn't mind if he didn't want to see us. I just needed to know he was not lying comatose on the floor.

After another twenty minutes Maria and I finally gave up. Together we got into the car and started to drive back to Wandsworth. Maria was convinced that Bill had been there.

Just as we drove over Wandsworth Bridge, my mobile went off. Maria picked it up for me and held it to my ear. It was Bill.

'Clare, I've just come back from the shops,' he said, sounding calm and rational enough. 'I'd only been out for five minutes. I can't believe I missed you. I'm so sorry. Here I am stuck all on my own, not seeing anyone for days and then two people I really want to see come round and I'm not here.'

I didn't ask how he knew we had been there, did not want to embarrass him. It was enough in that moment to know that he was alive.

'Shall we come back, Bill? I've got all this shopping for you.'

'No, don't worry, I feel a bit tired . . . think I'll lie down for a while. I've got some stuff in now anyway.'

'Are you sure, Bill? I'm worried you're not eating.'

'You are always worried, Clare. But don't, really, not about me. I'm fine . . .'

The last time I ever heard my brother's voice was a phone conversation we had two days later, around six o'clock in the evening of Sunday 27 November 2000.

I told Bill that I would be out of touch until late the following night – I had to go to Bristol for the day on business. Christy was coming with me – it was his birthday and we had planned to have lunch together. A friend had kindly agreed to pick Joseph up from nursery, give him supper, and stay with him until we got back. I was looking forward to it, felt Christy and I needed a day's break from worrying about Bill.

My brother sounded calm, unusually soft-voiced and gentle. He guessed my thought before I spoke it:

'I know you think I've been drinking,' he said. 'But I really haven't this time, I promise. Not for days now . . .'

A sudden rush both of fear and intense love for him prompted me to say: 'It's not that, Bill. It's everything. I'm just so terrified. I don't understand what's happening. You are just . . .' I hesitated to find the right words, 'not like yourself any more.'

'Don't, Clare,' Bill's voice sounded suddenly panicky, 'You're frightening me . . .'

There was a pause, before he said, 'I have been thinking about it myself. And I have worked it out. It took me a long time to get this way, so I guess it's going to take me a long time to get better again. But I will, I'm determined. I'm trying . . .'

'I will call you as soon as we get back tomorrow, Bill,' I told him reassuringly. 'You'll be there, won't you? It should be around eight.'

'Of course. Don't worry. Have a good time. And Clare . . .'

'What, Bill?'

'I love you.'

'I love you too, Bill . . .'

I rang that evening, but there was no answer. I rang again the next day. The following morning Christy and I broke into the Anselm Road flat to find his body.

Christy telephoned *The Times* that evening to tell old friends and colleagues. They seemed heartbroken. The obituaries desk rang back soon afterwards to clear up some points. Bill's obit ran the next morning. BBC Radio News picked it up from the first edition and made an announcement in their main bulletins.

'Versatile and sensitive reporter who covered many of the world's flashpoints for the BBC and *The Times*,' the obituary in his own newspaper was straplined.

'Frost's great strength was that he could grasp a complicated issue and render it intelligible for the lay reader . . . thorough, accurate and streetwise, after covering the general election of 1997, Frost moved from news to features where he continued to make a distinctive contribution to *The Times* until health problems led to his leaving the paper 18 months ago.'

It ended, as obituaries always end, with that cruel, clue-filled précis of any public personality's inner life: 'Bill Frost's marriage was dissolved. He was found dead yesterday aged 50.'

* * *

'We saw that in the office,' Customs investigator Anil Gogna told me at the end of our Treasury meeting. 'Bill Frost – dead. It gave us quite a jolt . . .'

But Bill's death had not stopped their assets recovery investigation. The matter of the Paul and Shark briefcase was at last explained. Customs had found Bill's 'address' on the police computer database, so Mike Torpy would tell me, the one he had given on the drink-driving arrest in February 2000 after the night when he had met Barbara Jones in London and smashed up his car.

The address was that of our cousin Sheilagh Frost's cottage in Sussex. It took Customs months and months to track down where Bill really lived – they apparently did not know about Anselm Road until a few days before his death, when they made their plans to 'interview' him at the flat.

But at the end there was nothing there – no paperwork, no evidence of laundered millions – nothing but my brother's dead body and the debris of addiction. I can only assume that the police who broke in with Christy told their Customs colleagues that. On 1 December they knew he was dead anyway, they read it in *The Times*, and it was running on the BBC news. It was too late to 'interview' my brother. If there was any 'evidence', Bill must have dropped it off somewhere along the way.

Thus it was that our kindly, harmless cousin Sheilagh had also been 'raided' a few days after Bill's death. After all, hers was his last known address – the police computer said so. She had been too discreet or too case-hardened by years as a south London GP to have said anything about it to me or other family members at the time, and so it remained for four years afterwards. With the greatest reluctance, she eventually told me what had happened when the Customs knock came on her cottage door.

Yes, Bill Frost had stayed with her, she had told her inquisitors. Yes, he had left some effects at her house – in particular, a case full of papers. But at Bill's funeral she had given it to his sister, his next-of-kin, Mrs Clare Campbell of Wandsworth. They, armed with a search warrant, found my address pretty easily, and so they had come knocking on my door a few days before Christmas. And I thought they were carol singers.

A few weeks after the Customs raid, I went to see Bill's bank manager to wind up what was left of his affairs. In fact, it was he who first contacted me – Alan Green, the kindly man who had found the redeemable insurance policy with which Bill had rented Anselm Road. He rang me very soon after Bill died – he had heard about his death on the radio, read the obituary in *The Times*, already been in touch with Barbara Jones, who had introduced her then lover to him as a client in the first place.

'It's a sad business, Clare,' he said in our phone conversation, 'and a terrible waste of such a talented man. You'll need help sorting out his affairs for a start. There was no will, of course, so you will have to apply for probate. Perhaps you should come and see me here. I have some personal effects of your brother's. There is very little money. He seems to have got through most of it before he died.' That much I knew already.

A month or so later I found myself sitting in Alan Green's London office. Together we worked through the pathetic pile of statements and cheque stubs, Bill's former bank manager deftly assembling them ready for the shredder. 'Here, let me help you with that, we don't have any more need of these,' he said, clearly conscious of my grief. He was soothing, gracious. But something had happened since the last time we talked on the phone. My house had been raided. I guessed in that moment that if Customs had been investigating my brother, investigating me, they must at some stage have contacted his bank. Tentatively I said: 'Before we destroy Bill's stuff, I have to ask you, Alan, has anyone else been here to see it?'

My host looked embarrassed. 'Yes,' he said as if reading my mind. 'I am sure you understand, Clare, that if HM C&E or the police demand to see a customer's bank statements, I'm obliged to comply whether I want to or not.'

When had the investigators been to rifle through his accounts? Was it when Bill was alive or afterwards? On that day so soon after my brother's death, I did not think to ask Alan that question.

'They did not find anything incriminating if that is any

comfort,' he said. Right then it was. Then Alan told me he was 'certain Bill would not have got involved with people like that' if his mind had been 'well, less disturbed'. I hated that remark, but had to agree.

'People like that' – what had he meant? There had been nothing about Hanley in the papers at the time, hardly anything about the Organisation. All I could assume was that Customs were telling him more than they were telling me.

'There was one thing, Clare, I needed to ask you about,' Alan said suddenly. 'The £20,000 he lent you in 1997. He said at the time you needed to borrow some money after your son was born . . .'

I bridled immediately. 'No, Alan. Bill never lent me £20,000. I never borrowed any money from my brother. There must be some mistake.'

'Well, that was what he told me anyway. So where, I wonder, did that money go? And, more importantly, who to?' I thought I might know.

There was one document in Bill's effects I found particularly distressing – his Switch card statement for the last weeks of his life, a computer print-out of automated self-destruction. It was horrible, horrible – but there was a crumb of comfort along the way.

Payments for food, to Pizza Hut or Iceland, stopped on 7 November 2000. There was a cash withdrawal in Barnes, south-west London, shortly afterwards – it must have been a Priory follow-up. For two weeks after that, it was Hair of the Dog, Hair of the Dog – the garish off-licence on the corner of Anselm Road: the sum of £18.23, two or sometimes three times a day, the price of a litre-bottle of Stolichnaya vodka.

And there it was, a six-day break from the 21st, a few days before Maria and I tried to see him with our tins of soup. He was telling me the truth, I thought, in that last telephone conversation. He was trying, trying to stay clean. Then, so the coldly impartial statement showed, there was another pay-out for 2 litres of vodka in Fulham sometime on the 28th. It was the anniversary of our father's death, and two years to the day since Kevin Hanley was arrested.

I think he couldn't take it – his body or his mind. I think that was the day Bill died.

Bill's death did not cause a ripple in the main trial still underway in what was still effectively total secrecy that winter of 2000–1. Counsel for the prosecution stated the Crown's case with plummy precision:

'The defendants represent the South American drug suppliers, those who move the drugs and the UK-based purchasers and distributors,' said the prosecuting counsel in his opening remarks. 'Because of the nature of the operation, massive financial resources were required, international travel and communication, and a vast network of contacts. The evidence which you will hear in this case is all about the arrangements for buying, transporting and receiving these cargoes.

'The Crown here allege that each of the defendants in this case, as well as others not in court, played their respective parts in trying to achieve their object, namely smuggling into this country a lot of illegal drugs and making a huge profit for themselves in the process . . .'

Bill had not made a 'a huge profit' out of any of it. His house, his earnings, seemed to have vanished. 'They bled him dry, didn't they,' the Customs investigator Mike Torpy had told me, 'that was my impression anyway.'

Here was the heart of the matter, my greatest problem. Had Bill been cynically picked clean? Bill had himself indicated to me at his lowest point that that was his own overwhelming fear. He was a stooge, his love for Alex in vain.

Had he really been fed drugs in return for acting as a respectable front man for Alex's brother as Customs investigators had suggested to me? If so, Kevin Hanley was a moral monster. The idea angered me in the moment beyond reason. But then as I considered it, wasn't it more true to the real world that Bill, at heart a romantic, had just gone crazy, showering the object of his obsession and her family with favours as a way of affirming his love?

He had taken Alex's son Louis to lunch once, I knew from Alex, and just paid for more and more champagne as afternoon turned into evening. He offered to stand bail for Lena, a quarter of a million pounds – except in the end of course he did not have it. It was a sad, mad, desperate gesture. He had paid for the Pagham caravan, he seemed to have paid for Kevin's family house, paid for lavish holidays – what was that all about? Was it money-laundering? None of the money seemed to have stuck to Bill.

Reluctantly, I did some accounting – began to look at what my brother had left behind. In his confessional at the Priory, he had answered the question 'How much has your drinking/drug use cost you?' as '£150,000 (approx)'. Drugs had evidently not come free. He had been paying market rates.

At the same time, he had formally written up in a Priory therapy session the steps he had to take to get 'clean': 'I must avoid wet places and wet people,' Bill wrote. 'I will tell my dealer who lives nearby that I am no longer a user.'

Kevin Hanley had lived nearby, but when Bill wrote that, Kevin had been in prison for almost two years. If I discovered Hanley at any point had been supplying Bill with drugs, I would cheerfully have torn him to pieces. One day, I thought, one day – I might just get the chance to ask him.

On 26 July 2001, eight months after Bill's death, verdicts were finally reached at the main trial held at Woolwich. Ronaldo Soares, Brian Wright junior, Ian Kiernan, Paul Shannon and Paul Rodgers had all pleaded not guilty to the charge of conspiracy to import and supply cocaine.

The jury found differently. Ronaldo Soares was sentenced to twenty-four years in prison, Brian Wright junior to sixteen. The 'gofer' Ian Kiernan got twenty. Paul Shannon, the Milkman's former son-in-law, got six years. The hapless yachtsman Paul Rodgers (later described exultingly by *The Sun* as an 'ex-*Daily Mirror* journalist') got nineteen years. Roger Newton, the strange Essex 'carpenter', and Barry Fennell, who I had met on that mad day outside Bill's house, pleaded guilty to possession with intent to supply. Newton and Fennell were sentenced to nine and ten years respectively.

The racehorse-owning comedian Jim Davidson appeared as a character witness for Wright's son 'Briany'. In spite of the entertainer's intervention, the jury found Brian Wright junior guilty. He got sixteen years.

The taxi driver Mick O'Connor of Fulham was acquitted, as was the Marbella-based businessman and the yachtsman Roman Smolen. Gary Boshoff was never caught.

On 7 August 2001 Kevin Hanley, the 'lieutenant, not the general' as his defence counsel had described him at the committal hearing, was sentenced to fifteen years for conspiracy to import and supply.

The ex-jockey Barrie Wright pleaded not guilty at his trial at Southampton, and the jury, concurred. His fellow jockey Graham Bradley appeared as a defence witness – sensationally admitting that both he and the defendant had accepted money from 'Uncle' Brian for passing on inside information on horses. Bradley said of Wright: 'It's exaggerating only a bit to say that he always carries a roll of notes with him that would choke a donkey.'

The jury in Hilton van Staden's case heard at Bristol could not reach a verdict. A retrial was ordered. Until that had concluded, everything about Operation Extend, the convictions and the acquittals, would remain secret.

Judith Parks was arrested in the US Virgin Islands in August 2001. Like her fellow American seafarers, James Goodrich and James Ewart, she seemed ready at the end to co-operate with her accusers. At first she had denied it all apparently, until Customs investigators confronted her with a video rental card from a shop near Pagham that they found in her possessions. It was in the name of Kevin Hanley.

Intimate details of the 1996 *Selina* mission with Hanley and Hoppenbrouwers came out in her testimony – as did the re-run in 1998 when she was aboard another coopering vessel, the *Ramarch*, with Hanley supervising the reception of the cargoes ashore. Her evidence was too late, however, to be used to secure the English convictions.

But Judith Parks did give evidence against the grizzled Dutchman 'Pappy' Hoppenbrouwers at his Miami trial in

Autumn 2001. He was sentenced to thirty years and Judith Parks herself to eight. In early June 2002 she was flown to England to give evidence against Hilton van Staden at his retrial at Bristol Crown Court. This time he pleaded guilty and was sentenced to nine years.

It was over – almost. On 14 June 2002 the press embargo on Operation Extend and the trials that followed was at last lifted. With its monster scale and fugitive 'Mr Big', the story was a gift to newspaper crime correspondents: 'One of the biggest British drug smuggling rings has been smashed by Customs officers,' reported the *Daily Mail*. 'But the mastermind behind the gang, which is believed to have flooded this country with at least £500 million worth of cocaine, has escaped justice, it emerged yesterday.

'Brian Wright is wanted on an international arrest warrant but remains a free man because he is hiding in Northern Cyprus which has no extradition treaty with this country.

'Until now the smooth-talking gambler, who boasted a celebrity lifestyle, could not be named because of a contempt order during a series of trials which destroyed his vast drugs empire . . .'

The *Cyprus Mail* reported soon afterwards: '[Wright] lives in a £300,000 villa surrounded by imposing gates and 10-foot walls near occupied Lapithos, eight miles west of Kyrenia.

'Wright bought the house in the name of a Turkish Cypriot friend . . . The fugitive regularly changes the numbers of his mobile phones, which are not registered in his name for security reasons. His wife Josie, whom he married at the age of 19, now rarely visits him abroad. He is said to feel guilty about fleeing while his associates – including his own son – were serving time.'

The *Guardian* carried a report from Athens a month later: '[Wright], fearing he was about to be sent to Turkey which does have an extradition treaty with Britain, slipped into the Greek-controlled south of the island, reportedly landing in Paphos in a fishing boat. His villa outside Kyrenia and BMW car were both found abandoned.

'The hunt for Mr Big has been made all the more difficult

because of its undercover nature,' the story continued. 'Wright, say British officials, will probably lie low – if he hasn't radically changed his appearance – until he wangles false travel documents . . .'

On 19 March 2005 someone sent me a text message telling me to get that day's *Daily Mail*. There was a half-page story buried deep on page 39: 'Milkman's run comes to end with arrest in southern Spain. A fugitive accused of masterminding one of Britain's biggest drug-smuggling operations and fixing hundreds of horse races has finally been arrested after six years on the run.

'Brian Wright, 58, was seized in Marbella, southern Spain. He was tracked down to the Costa del Sol following an intelligence operation by Britain's Customs and Excise.'

I think I had always been rather frightened of 'Uncle' Brian out there somewhere on a Mediterranean verandah with his millions tucked away, whispering orders into a mobile phone. I was not quite so frightened now.

34

On a cold, bright spring morning a few weeks after the news of Wright's arrest, I met Alex Hanley. We had been in touch only once or twice in the almost five years since Bill had died. She had called me, as Barbara and Ruth had done, on the first anniversary of Bill's death in a spirit of solidarity – as if to share the sorrow of a mutual bereavement.

After that I had heard nothing – until a sudden flurry of calls in early 2005 about photographs. Alex had found some of Bill taken on a holiday in the Caribbean. He had been happy then and looked fit and well, she said. Would I like some copies? Yes, I would very much. I had only very few pictures of Bill and those dated back to childhood or adolescence.

Alex had eventually sent them in the post. I copied them on to my computer and called her to suggest we might meet so I could return them in person. She agreed. I mentioned to her idly that I might be writing a book about Bill – after all, writing is what I do.

Now we were to meet again. I was not looking forward to it. I had some very difficult questions to ask.

I felt ridiculously nervous as I parked my car down a side street off Wandsworth Bridge Road, hands shaking as I switched off the engine. The whole place reminded me of Bill's last years – meeting him in the same coffee shop where I was now to meet Alex. Joe's Café – the wine bar where Bill had once sat with me, serially ordering Bloody Marys – was just a few doors down. I glanced through the window of a nearby Italian restaurant, where even the pink napkins evoked memories of panicky lunches as Bill sat over plates of uneaten food.

Arriving early and not wanting to be the first, I went into a newsagent to waste time. When I came out I caught sight of a woman sitting down at the front of the café, black-leather biker's jacket, off-white scarf and blue jeans. It was Alex.

We greeted one another warmly. In spite of all that had happened, I felt pleased to see her – partly through relief that she had turned up at all, and partly because of everything that we had been through together. It was not Alex's fault that Bill had died.

We immediately began exchanging family updates as all women and mothers do. Yes, Katy and Maria were fine. Joseph was now eight, a happy little boy now taller than his friends by several inches. He looked a lot like his father – often reminding me of Bill too, of course.

Louis, Alex's eldest son, was now living in Norfolk and hoping to make a career as an artist and had already had some success. Max was now twenty-one and living in a residential home. He would never get any better, Alex told me flatly. But she visited him often and frequently brought him home to her flat in Shepherds Bush for weekends. Bridget had just celebrated her eightieth birthday. Another of Alex's brothers, Brian, a heroin addict, had died a year after Bill. Right now, Alex did not have a man in her life – she had never met anyone, she claimed, who came near to replacing Bill.

'You just don't meet someone with a mind like Bill's . . . or as funny. Or who had looks like he did,' she said. 'He had it all.'

Yes, he did, I thought. Now I felt was the right time to reveal what I knew – what I had found out since Bill's death.

'You didn't know about the Customs raid, Alex? What happened to us afterwards?' I said softly.

Her face froze: 'No!'

'They came to see us . . . with a search warrant . . . two weeks after the funeral. They told me Bill was involved with Kevin, money-laundering for him . . .'

Alex looked horrified, tried to stop me from speaking. But I motored on, determined to say my piece:

'We didn't know, Alex,' I said. 'Well, I knew Kevin had been arrested of course. But I thought he was just a dinner party dealer. Nothing ever on this scale.'

Then I asked her directly: 'Did you know, Alex? Did you know Bill was doing things for Kevin?'

'No! Clare, I am certain he wasn't. This is wrong. It has to be. I swear to you, none of the family knew the sort of trouble Kevin had got himself into.'

She was talking rapidly now, too fast for me to interrupt.

'Kevin was only thirty when he first got involved with Wright, a Fulham lad who thought it was glamorous to hang round with these people. He didn't realise he was going to be dealing with Colombian drugs cartels. He was as scared as you or I would be. I promise . . . But as for Bill, that's just plain wrong. I'm sure it didn't happen . . .'

'Yes, Alex,' I replied firmly. 'It did. I have the lease agreement for the caravan in Pagham. It was in the briefcase he left at my cousin's house in Sussex. Customs have told me he was leasing other property too, a house in Bishops Road.'

'The caravan was Lena's! Nothing to do with drugs.'

'Well, that's not what customs told me,' I replied. 'They seemed to know all about it.'

Alex looked shocked.

'Clare, have you really thought this through?' she said. 'What exactly is this book going to be about? Do you really think this is what Bill would have wanted? You have to think about that, too. You owe it to him.'

I owe it to Bill to write the truth, I thought. But I did not say it to Alex. Not then.

'Would Kevin talk to me?' I asked. Alex hesitated, thinking quickly, not answering my question. 'He's been decategorised – about to be moved from York to the Isle of Sheppey,' she said. 'We went to the High Court, the whole family. Kevin's a changed man, he really is. He regrets all of this so much.'

What about Bill, I thought in silence. Did he regret that?

Alex could have been reading my mind. 'Kevin didn't understand addiction,' she said. 'Not before he went into jail anyway. But he does now. He's met addicts in there and has worked as a

Samaritan with them. He's so different you wouldn't recognise him. He's been told the prison officers don't want him moved to another prison. They don't want to lose him, he's such a calming influence on the others . . .'

I changed the subject to the recent arrest of Kevin's former boss. Alex looked angry, not at me, but at the mention of the man she felt had led her brother astray.

'Wright stitched them all up – his own son Briany included,' she said. 'He bribes everybody – that's how he gets away with it. You have no idea, Wright has influence everywhere . . . very high-up people too. Kevin has told them all in prison what Wright's like. You don't do that unless it's true. You don't take the risk of lying when you're in there. Whatever else Kevin may be, he's not a liar.'

I cut across her: 'Why did Bill stand bail for Lena? Who made him do that? They told me he broke down in court he was in such a state.'

'Bill wanted to!' Alex snapped back. She was indignant now, angry. 'He liked Lena! Anyway, in the end he didn't have the money. Someone else paid it. He spent the night before with me. The reason he collapsed in court was because he'd been drinking the night before, got himself into a right state. You know what he could be like. He wasn't that bad in court that day anyway, just a bit shaky . . .'

She trailed off, realising how callous this sounded. A certain amount of contrition began to creep in.

'Of course, I have asked myself a thousand times . . .' The unspoken thought hung in the air between us. I myself knew what she meant, the constant self-questioning – could either of us have done anything to save him, or was disaster inevitable? She seemed to think it might have been all along.

'Bill had problems long before I ever met him,' she continued. 'He was sitting in that house alone with the headphones on . . . getting out of it. When I met him again after all those years, I wasn't even sure at first that I wanted to go out with him. He wasn't looking after himself properly even then.'

Her eyes looked down. I stared back, trying not to look

accusing. I must have failed. What about the time in that horrible basement in Oxford Gardens, I thought, the descent into hell. Once again, she must have read my mind.

'You know I never knew anything about the crack?' she said. I wasn't going to press her about what she really knew – and I supposed what she had to say next was true:

'I didn't have a clue where Bill got it from. I just went over to see him in Notting Hill that day and found him with a black eye. God knows what he was up to, or with who. But it was nothing to do with me. The sort of people who deal in crack are something else. Nothing like coke dealers.'

Perhaps they weren't. I wasn't going to argue about the finer moral points of drug-dealing. We carried on like this for another hour, tentatively trading information. There was no hostility, just a wariness on both sides. She naturally wanted to protect her own brother and I wanted to know what had really happened to mine. Finally, she got to it.

'Clare, I really think you should talk to Kevin,' she said. 'Give him a chance to have his say. It's not fair otherwise, not if you are planning to paint him as the villain in all of this . . .'

'OK, Alex,' I said. 'That's what I really want to do – to talk to Kevin. When can I see him?'

We parted outside the café, a quick embrace, 'I'll call you' – and Alex was gone.

35

She did call me. A 'visitor's order' arrived by courier a month after our meeting. Alex had fixed it. The delay was not her fault – after six and a half years, Kevin had indeed been decategorised from a high-security prison, Full Sutton at York, and moved in the meantime to the supposedly softer 'B rating' of HM Prison Swaleside on the Isle of Sheppey in Kent. Kevin, it seemed, was very prepared to see me – to set the record straight.

Arriving at the nearest station, Sheerness, I approached a taxi. The driver was polishing the boot of his cab.

'Can you take me to the prison?'

Without looking up, he grunted: 'Get in.'

Visitors to Swaleside clearly did not merit an excess of politeness. We drove in silence for miles. Approaching the prison, I asked my driver if he could collect me afterwards. For the first time, he turned round to inspect me properly. Scanning my blue linen suit, he said: 'You a brief, then?'

'No, a journalist. But that's not why I am here. I've come to see a . . . friend. I don't know how long I'll be . . .'

'Doesn't make any difference when you want to leave. You can't until visiting times are over. Sometimes they let you out at four, sometimes quarter-past.'

Two women prison officers were sitting on the wall in front of the visitors' registration office, a brick hut outside the main perimeter. I asked them where I had to go. They looked me up and down before smirking at one another and nodding to me to follow them. I had my left hand stamped with some kind of fluorescent ink and was handed a locker key.

'Over there – all your belongings. Nothing to be taken in or out . . .'

I sat down, one among a crowd of families and girlfriends. In the ladies' room I found female solidarity with three teenage girls applying their make-up. 'You don't want to pay no attention to those bitches on the door,' one remarked: 'This is your first time, isn't it? Don't worry. You stick with us. We'll look after you . . .'

We shuffled in a file past rolls of barbed wire through clanging gates into the prison itself – with a body search even for the smallest children and babies. My heart lurched as we reached the visiting room; it looked like an old-fashioned cafeteria with rows of alphabetically marked small tables and chairs screwed into the floor.

We each gave our numbers and were allocated to a table. '174? Kevin Hanley? . . . B5, love,' said a grizzled but kindly male warder.

All around me couples were embracing, children being swung into the air and kissed. Only I stood alone, staring at the empty seat in front of me that should have contained Kevin Hanley. I waited and I waited. Had he at the last refused to see me? It was a security check apparently – a routine head count of prisoners.

Suddenly a door opened at the other end of the room. A smiling, stockily built man in his mid-forties accompanied by an officer walked in. Our eyes met. It was Kevin.

He strode forward, putting his arms round me to kiss me on both cheeks.

'Clare. I'm so sorry . . . I really am . . .'

I smiled back nervously.

'Thanks for seeing me, Kevin. I had to know, you understand? Find out what happened, how much Bill was involved. After the Customs raid I could not just leave things . . .'

'Clare, you have to believe me. I knew nothing about that until Alex told me last week,' he said. Kevin's indignation seemed directed at Customs rather than the train of events that led them to my door. 'They had no right to raid you like that,' he said. 'Makes me angry. You were respectable people – nothing to do with all this . . .'

It was all tumbling out in a rush. Here was someone who could tell me everything if he chose to. Warders cruised past the table like exam invigilators. The burning question, how much did Bill know, hung unspoken in the air.

'He wasn't involved, I promise you,' said Kevin unprompted by me. 'He knew I was up to some sort of skullduggery, of course, but not the details. He never asked and anyway I wouldn't have told him. I would never have got him involved. We were just mates, that was all. I loved that man. After all, he was my sister's boyfriend. Good as gold he was, good as gold. And always such a laugh, too . . .'

'But Kevin, there was a search warrant. Bill's name and yours together. There was mention of money-laundering. And then in the briefcase they took from me there were papers, a rental agreement for the caravan at Pagham. Bill told me he did that because he owed you money.'

Kevin looked suddenly nervous; I carried on, determined not to give him an easy ride:

'And there was Bishops Road, the house that Customs told me Bill leased for you. Why did he do that, Kevin, why if he was nothing to do with any of this?'

Stammering slightly now, Kevin replied: 'That was nothing. Look, I'm not pretending. I admit I was up to no good. I've never had a mortgage or a bank account in my life. I couldn't give the references they wanted. But Bill was a reporter, worked for *The Times*. He had all the credentials you could ask for. So he said he would take out the lease for me . . . he was a good bloke like that. We were mates after all . . . You have to understand, Clare. I did what I did and now I'm serving time for it. But I never involved the people around me. Not Bill, not Alex, not Lena. That's it . . .'

'But Lena was arrested,' I said. 'What was she supposed to have done? And Bill stood bail for her – when he was really bad. Why?'

'He wanted to help. Customs were putting pressure on me to change my plea to guilty. I wouldn't, so they hit on Lena. Harry was only a baby. I was desperate to protect Lena and my kids...'

'How much did Bill put up?' I asked. 'He didn't have any money by then, I know . . .'

'Two hundred and fifty grand, I think it was. But when it came to it, he let me down . . . I got a call from my brief to say Bill didn't have the money. I could have said something then but I didn't. As I said, he was a good bloke. But by then he was lagged most of the time. The prison officers used to have a laugh when he came in to see me with his tie all crooked and stinking of drink. Shouldn't have let him in really like that, but they did.'

'But why, Kevin, why was he drunk like that whenever he came to see you? Bill got much worse after you were arrested. Perhaps he was scared that he would be next . . .'

'No, no, Clare, nothing like that – I keep telling you . . .'

'But, Kevin, he told me certain things himself. Like the time you were hiding out in Wiseton Road . . . you'd been beaten up with baseball bats . . .'

Kevin smiled, dismissing the incident with a wave.

'Oh that . . . I wasn't exactly hiding. These things happen in my line of business. I couldn't walk very well for about a week afterwards, but it was no big deal. Perhaps Bill was over-dramatising.'

'And the gun, Kevin? What about that? Bill told me there was a gun hidden in the garden at Wiseton Road . . .'

Kevin's features hardened suddenly, his eyes narrowing as he looked at me.

'There was no gun, Clare . . . Absolutely not. Bill must have been fantasising.'

I could see Kevin backing off, now suddenly aware that I knew far more than he had thought I did. I tried a different tack: 'What about you, Kevin. How did you get into it yourself? When did you first meet Brian Brendon Wright?'

'What's he got to do with this?'

'Well, Kevin. It was in the papers.'

'It's rubbish, all of it, Clare,' he said urgently. 'What they say about Wright. None of it's true, not the papers, not the TV programme – not a word of it . . .'

'Did Bill ever meet him?' I asked. 'Did he ever meet, who is it, Ronald Soares?'

Kevin twitched. 'No. no, not ever, he never met any of those people . . .'

'But you know Wright's been arrested, coming up for trial next year . . .'

My mention of Wright had sent a chill through the conversation. This was not going to get me anywhere. Kevin spelled out the rules: 'Look, Clare. I said I would see you as Bill's sister because I was sorry that you and your brother had ever been dragged into all this. You didn't deserve to be. But I'm just not prepared to talk to you about Wright or any of the rest of it. Christ, this is worse than the bloody police interview. I don't know who has been filling your head with this stuff . . .'

'No one, Kevin,' I said quietly. 'I found out . . . I'm a reporter. It's what I do. And it's what Bill did before he got so bad.'

The most difficult question of all was coming. I forced him to make eye contact with me: 'Did you supply him, Kevin?' I asked, my own voice hardening now. 'Did you supply him, Kevin?' I repeated softly.

'No, I swear. I know what it looks like. Here I was sitting on tons of cocaine and him an addict. But it wasn't like that. We were mates, like I keep saying. I'm not a small-time dealer, 1 or 2 grams here and there. I'm only into the big stuff . . . Bill had his own people . . .'

I was prepared to believe him.

'And the crack? Do you know where he got that?'

'Jesus, I didn't know that he was on that stuff until you said it. I know Alex suspected, but it was nothing to do with me . . .'

'Alex says you didn't understand addiction before you came into prison?'

'Yes, that's true. I didn't realise about Bill. I knew he liked a drink. But I thought he was like me about charlie. That he could do a line and then leave it . . . Look, Clare, I know it's terrible for you to have lost him,' Kevin said suddenly. 'But it's time to move on. Other people do.' Kevin pointed round the room. 'People in here have lost friends, relatives . . . lost all track of their own lives. But they come out and pick up the pieces. Look ahead to the future like I am . . .'

'What will you do when you come out?' I asked.

'Try the best I can to make it up to my family . . . the kids for the time we've lost together. Look, I wish you all the best with the book, but don't go filling it with a pack of lies about me please . . .'

The clock showed a few minutes to four. Prison officers were rounding up their charges amid tearful farewells. A small boy about my own son's age had his face pressed up against the glass partition nearest us, crying in the direction of his retreating father's back.

'Goodbye, Kevin. Thanks again for talking to me,' I said. 'And good luck yourself.'

We stood up together, hesitating, before both holding our arms towards one another. Kevin Hanley hugged me close to him. It occurred to me that a watching stranger might have taken us for brother and sister. I kissed him back – guessing that was the way Bill would have wanted it.

Five years after my brother's death I went to the suburban cemetery in south London on a cold November day and remembered the turmoil that had surrounded his funeral – Bill's rival lovers tear-streaked behind dark glasses, the solemn throng of journalists, my own mix of anger and overwhelming grief.

I was alone this time. The world had moved on – new dramas, new human disasters, plenty of new stories on which Bill might have reported.

What did I know? What had I learned from my journey into the mirror-world? Who really was to blame for Bill's death? I had not found a single culprit – but a combination of toxic elements that had finally and fatally come together.

I could not now believe, if I ever really had, that Bill had been 'killed' by anyone in particular. Drugs had done for him, I was certain of that. But so had Bill's addictive personality that for so long had led him to seek out risk and danger from Beirut to Bosnia. Kevin's doings provided a debased substitute for all of that.

But knowing what I now knew – the whole, mad business of the

cocaine conspiracy and its Goonish cast of middle-aged villains –
I understood a little bit better what my brother must have been
feeling. He would have found it banal and terrifying all at once.
He had not been part of it, I know that. He had known about
much of it, I am sure, he was too good a reporter not to, but once
he was in the mirror-world there was no coming back.

I only wish that he had told me more. Bill and I had always
shared everything together from childhood. But this was one
place my brother had gone where I could not follow – and nor
did he want me to. 'Don't ask,' he had whispered to me in life,
'you don't want to go there.' In death I had disobeyed his
instruction.

In his professional career Bill broadcast and wrote about what
happens to other people – hardly ever himself. I don't know what
he would have thought about his sister setting out to tell his story.
I just wished he were still alive to tell it himself.

36

On 2 May 2006, Christy and I took an early-morning minicab to southeast London to witness the arraignment of Brian Brendon Wright alongside Kevin's former mistress, Anni Rowland, at Woolwich Crown Court. They were an odd couple, united only in being accused of cocaine crime. They ignored each other. He was supposed to be some sort of master criminal. She was the single mother to Kevin's now nine-year-old son. I had last seen her in 1998 on a summer's morning in Wiseton Road when Bill had introduced her to me as 'Kevin's girlfriend'. She was that and more. At the time I thought her a pretty blonde in her thirties, very similar in style to Lena, Kevin's wife. Now she stood in a courtroom flanked by female prison warders.

The place itself was modern and bright with strange acoustics which, combined with the archaic formality of the lawyers' language, added to the feeling we were all taking part in a piece of elaborate theatre. Sitting down in the central well of the court alongside the clerks and solicitors, I found myself just yards from the glass-screened defendants. Anni seemed nervous, shaken and pale. Brian Wright was smart-suited, tanned and smiling. Had I not known that he had been held in custody first in Malaga and then, following his extradition in high security Belmarsh, for the previous twelve months, I would never have believed this man had been in prison at all. His family grinned and gurned from the public gallery. The legal preliminaries seemed interminable. I left the court that day weary and disheartened. 'Closure' was still a long way off.

Seven months later, just before Christmas 2006, Michael Torpy rang to say that Anni had pleaded guilty and had been sentenced to five years imprisonment. It was six years to the day that customs had first raided our home in search of our supposed involvement in drugs money laundering. The man who linked us all, Kevin Hanley, I knew to be himself on the brink of release on license from prison. Now it was the turn of his boss, if that is what he was, to face his accusers.

In February 2007 it began in earnest. It was a set piece for customs; they had to get this one right. Eleven years in the making, the trial of Brian Brendon Wright was not going to be routine. There were two charges, conspiracy to evade prohibition on the importation of a controlled drug, and conspiracy to supply. Government ministers had pinned their credibility on bringing the 'godfathers' of organised crime to justice. Under a new law, the Serious Organised Crime and Police Act, 2005, four witnesses who had themselves been previous players in the drama, were granted immunity from prosecution in this country. In reality, it was like being stuck at an airport. Armed police bristling with guns and body searches became routine. The Wright family (and some mysterious bubble-gum-chewing hangers-on), journalists and Home Office spooks would collide in the security 'air-lock' leading to Court Number One to be corralled together in the tiny public gallery. The lawyers had their own little room with coffee and chocolate cake. We all tried to be polite – even if there was some effing and blinding (but not from the journalists) as the prosecution laid out their case. An elderly man with a hearing aid growled 'fucking prove it', every time Brian Wright's alleged misdeeds were mentioned. Customs witnesses were all 'fucking liars'. The jury were masked from public view in a huge plywood box. Sometimes I wished I could be too.

Wright's daughter, Joanne, blonde and smiling, and his eighteen-year-old grandson listened intently – as men with boxers' faces dozed in the seats beside them through the more detailed evidence. Uncle Brian beamed back giving his testimony from the witness box. He was confident, cocky, polite to the judge and scathing of the prosecution. He oozed menace and avuncular charm by turn. Jim Davidson took the stand to tell us of his horse-racing chum's generosity.

There was a special sadness for me as the trial got under way. Danny McGrory, Bill's colleague and friend at *The Times*, the one who has stayed loyal when others peeled away, died suddenly of a stroke. He was fifty-four years old.

The prosecution witnesses were an all-star cast – James Goodrich who gave an extraordinary account of a thirty-year 'secret life' as a professional drugs-runner, Godfried Hoppenbrouwers and Judith Parks – who had been flown in from the USA along with a man I'd never heard of before named Alex de Cubas. He had been high up in the Colombian drugs cartel – until he was extradited to the USA in 2000 and sentenced to thirty years.

De Cubas had been linked with a drugs overlord in Colombia called Victor Mejia. With an associate called Lester Delgado (the real name of the character I had come to know as 'Pinky'), de Cubas had set up shop in Brazil and opened contacts with customers in the USA and Europe. They soon realised the hungriest and most profitable cocaine market was Britain.

'Pappy' Hoppenbrouwers's testimony was the most damning. The grizzled yachtsman had come to frequent the Caribbean drug haven of St Maarten. His first involvement with drugs was sailing a boat stuffed with cannabis from the Dutch island to Boston for which he was paid $100,000. The Boston run had introduced him to 'Pinky'. The ageing Dutchman's dream apparently was to open a luxury hotel-brothel in the Brazilian port of Recife. He had, so he testified, sought investors through Pinky who in return asked him to collect drugs money from his associate Pedro Jiminez, also known as 'Flaco' who was, it seemed, based in Britain. Pappy had already transported cash and gold bars, cocaine profits, westwards across the Atlantic several times.

In 1995 Pappy arrived in England once more, so he testified. He rented a house at 11 Grange Road, Christchurch on the Hampshire coast. One day that summer, an associate of Pinky and Flaco (described by Hoppenbrouwers as 'a young Hispanic man') arrived at the house with a car and trailer load of cocaine – 300 kilos in total. According to the prosecution: 'It was at this point that Hoppenbrouwers became aware of the full nature of Pinky's dealings.' He insisted on secreting the cocaine in the adjoining garage. The drugs were to be moved to London in stages. Mr Hoppenbrouwers believed the young man was not up to the task 'so he himself took charge of delivering the drugs to Waterloo station . . . [into the care of Gary Boshoff, the South African who would feature in later drug-running missions].'

'With about 150 kilos remaining in the garage an Englishman arrived at the Christchurch house to collect the remainder . . . this was Hoppenbrouwers' first meeting with Kevin Hanley . . .' said the prosecution. So Kevin, according to this evidence, was already in the cocaine wholesale business in summer 1995. That was when Bill was in his first flush of mateyness with his 'brother-in-law', when he was partying like a twenty-five-year old, when he would disappear for long weekends to the Cotswolds and the New Forest.

The Colombian Alex de Cubas further told the court that he had dealt directly with Kevin in supplying a tonne of cocaine in 1998 which was smuggled on board the American registered yacht, the *Cyan*. So Kevin might not have been just the lowly 'lieutenant' after all. The deal with Anni and her movement of both cocaine and cash seemed out of everyone's sight – his wife Lena's certainly.

I remembered calls from Bill at the time telling me over and over again that the Hanley women were 'doing his head in' with their endless nattering about Kevin's affair. I also remembered how close Anni and Alex seemed – but as the sister of a philandering brother myself, I understood she had to be as sympathetic to Kevin's new partner as she had been to his wife.

Kevin's apparent going alone was the basis of Wright's defence. 'Uncle' was a family man, he loved children, he would never 'do drugs'. He spat the words out. It was all Kevin's operation, it always was, he knew nothing about it. It was Kevin who had sent money-bearing emissaries to the Caribbean, including the 'naïve' jockey, Barrie Wright. When 'Uncle' had found out he was furious. When Kevin was arrested and Lena had turned up on his doorstep at Chelsea Harbour at 2.30 am, she was simply turning to an old family friend for help, according to the defence. Anyway, he had sent Lena away.

As I heard that, I remembered that night with a cold anger. Bill, coked up, terrified, stumbling round our front room, storming out as he boastfully announced his intention of going to the 'Conrad Hotel'. Wright had known Kevin since he was fifteen, he said, he had watched him grow up. He and Lena had been to the house in Spain. He was shocked, shocked, to hear about his relationship with Anni Rowland.

What about the investigators' sighting of Wright and Hanley together in spring and summer 1998, the phone calls from anonymous telephone boxes in Kensington and Pimlico? That was about getting knockoff tickets for the World Cup final, according to his defence – that and arranging a flat for his girlfriend. Presented with evidence about a mountain of cash kept in someone's loft, Wright explained that it was the proceeds of gambling – everything was. There were no records, no bank accounts. He had never paid tax, never owned a house or car in his own name. Now he was worth nothing – 'zilch'. His explanations were very detailed – almost plausible.

Could it really have been Kevin all along? Godfried Hoppenbrouwer's evidence against Wright was harder to deny. In England in 1996 following the *Casita* mission – seeking investors for his Brazilian 'brothel' – he said that Kevin introduced him to a man who Hanley called 'Mr B'. The meeting took place in a fish-and-chip shop in Poole. It was Brian Brendon Wright.

There was another encounter with the man Kevin described as his 'boss' in October 1998. This time Pappy was in Paris – to float his brothel scheme once more. Wright was there, outlining a plan for an even bigger import operation to come the following year using a freighter that would be offloaded in the North Sea. The old sailor Pappy told him the weather was too unpredictable.

Wright denied everything, he'd never heard of Hoppenbrouwers, there had been no fish-and-chip shop meeting. He had been in Paris in October 1998, but for the Arc de Triomphe horse race. No cocaine shipping plans. The Dutchman was making it all up to get his sentence reduced.

Pappy's evidence and that of Alex de Cubas gave an insight into the crisis of Hanley's arrest which had thrown Bill into such turmoil. De Cubas testified that following the successful tranship-ments it was the Dutchman's role to ensure that the interests of the organisation in South America were protected by minding the drugs and distributing them in stages. 'But Hoppenbrouwers disobeyed this order and gave Hanley full control of the entire remaining cargo of drugs', he said. That had been a big mistake. Out of the blue, it seemed, Kevin had been arrested. The jury heard that after that 'the key to the movement of the cocaine was a woman who was very close to Kevin.'

Then Ronaldo Soares had flown in to rescue the cartel's cocaine. Wright denied ever meeting him. 'I was not at Sloane Square . . . I never knew Soares,' he insisted to the jury, 'At the time I was recuperating from a heart operation.'

The judges's summing up was a model of neutrality. The jury retired on the morning of Tuesday 27 March 2007. The little group of journalists covering the trial gossiped in the windowless press room. Wright's family kept their own vigil down the corri-dor. With the jury out, Customs produced a background state-ment embargoed for publication against a (guilty) verdict. It told me things I did not know – and which had not come out at the trial.

For example, Anni Rowland had been arrested at her home in Burford in the Costwolds in October 2005. 'Customs later learned that from as early as 1998 and continuing through to the time Hanley was in prison, Anni formed a fundamental role as Hanley's money launderer' the briefing document said dis-passionately. 'Anni also acted as a conduit for him while Kevin Hanley was in prison paying money to associates he met while in prison.' She was the one, it seemed, who had control of the cocaine and knew of its secret whereabouts when the great crisis had come in November 1998.

Upon her arrest almost seven years later, £49,000 in cash and £20,000 worth of gold coins were found – and 'numerous bank accounts were also identified – these revealed large amounts of unexplained deposits believed to be the proceeds of crime.'

The briefing paper also mentioned the hapless Brian Coldwell who took money to Sweden to pay for the Flex and to Geneva in 1998 for Anni to deposit in a numbered Swiss bank account. They stayed in the Hôtel d'Angleterre 'the most expensive in the city' Customs noted sniffily. It mentioned someone called 'Gary Dean Mace' of Coldicote Farm, Moreton-in-the-Marsh, also in the Cotswolds. He was described as 'an associate of Rowland' who safeguarded £110,000 of Kevin Hanley's drug money. 'He stated in an interview that he had given Anni Rowland back approximately £50,000. He said that he buried the remainder of the money under an oak tree. He maintains he now suffers from posttraumatic stress and cannot remember the tree.'

I looked at a map. Coldicote Farm, whatever that was, was half a mile from the lock-up from which I had retrieved Bill's forlorn furniture and a few family pictures four years earlier.

Days had passed and the jury was still out. In my head so was mine. I raged against these people with their sentimental facade of family loyalty. Perhaps Kevin really was the real villain of it all. Whatever I might think, it seemed that Wright, who had bet an arresting officer one pound to a million that the charges would never stick, might indeed walk free.

The weekend came and went. The judge indicated he would accept a majority verdict. The jury split ten to two. On Monday 2 April 2007 they delivered their decision in Court Number One. Guilty on both charges. Uncle Brian got thirty years.

Afterword

by Nick Charles, MBE, founder and director of the Chaucer Clinic ('Chaucer') in west London, who treated Bill for alcoholism in the early spring of 2000.

There were three alcoholics admitted to the Chaucer that day – 'Donald Duck', an Asian guy who said he was a doctor, 'Richard Branson', who said he was 'big in the city', and 'Bill Frost', who claimed to be a war correspondent. It was just an ordinary day for those in charge of admissions and they were quite used to the delusions of those who were alcoholically sick.

Donald Duck was indeed a doctor, just as he claimed. Mr Branson was a West Indian – but 'Bill Frost', well, he turned out to be Bill Frost the journalist.

After Bill had passed his assessment and subsequently been admitted, Nikki de Villier, Chaucer's General Manager, remarked on the cold stare with which he had greeted her. She thought his surname apt.

I remember sighing silently; I had treated journalists before and, although there were successes among them, they were a tough bunch and pretty much a law unto themselves.

Chaucer took people from all walks of life. There had been politicians, sportsmen, housewives, career girls, prostitutes and doctors – and many writers and journalists. I once asked Bill if he could give me a list of famous alcoholic writers for a piece I was writing. He told me it would be a lot easier than trying to give me a list of those who were not.

Bill didn't make many friends in the first forty-eight hours; in fact, I reprimanded one junior female member of staff who said she wished he'd simply 'bugger off'. I explained to her that the problem with drunks was you never knew why they drank to excess in the first place until you sobered them up.

Neither did you know how they were going to turn out. People who laughed all the way through the initial interview could be sullen and rude in sobriety. On the other hand, applicants we almost turned away in the first place because of their offensive behaviour transpired to be charming when they sobered up. Either way, it looked like Bill Frost was going to be trouble.

He had recently completed a course at an American clinic in Arizona, we knew that. It was 'a pretty useless place' according to Bill – and he had drunk champagne continually on the flight home, or so he admitted half-boastingly to staff. In fact, he arrived back in a worse state than when he had left. He seemed to foresee his stay with us as something similar – as somewhere to get 'fit' so he could drink again. Fair or not, any display of this sort of attitude was how staff judged patients on a daily basis in the early stages. The signs were not good.

Day four produced a surprise, Bill wanted to speak to me. Although I had a general rule not to spend too much time with patients when they were on detox medication, I agreed. A quite different persona presented itself in the Blue Room where we sat facing each other. He explained in a soft, well-educated voice that he had woken that day experiencing a strange peace.

I watched him walk down the long corridor back to the work therapy station and pause about halfway in order to allow a young woman patient, neatly dressed in kitchen attire, pass by with a heavy tray. He helped her with it, putting an arm gently around her shoulders to offer reassurance. The young woman, who would later cry uncontrollably at the news of Bill's death, had recently undergone major surgery. She would tell me some weeks later that he was the kindest man she had ever met.

He was winning affection from patients and staff. When during a group session it was Bill's turn to talk about the most enduring memory of his life, he had everyone's attention. Eager listeners waited to hear about famous criminal trials or dangerous war zones. Bill instead related a story from his childhood, a wonderfully descriptive account of a long-gone family seaside holiday at a place called Birchington in Kent, sand and sunshine and dabbling in rock-pools with his sister in another life.

Bill often mentioned the impossibility of explaining the complexities of alcohol addiction to those around him – lovers, family, colleagues, who themselves could not know. It might have helped, he said, if he had understood it himself. I sympathised – it was like men attempting to describe the pains of childbirth. The only genuine empathy came from those who had been there. I could count myself as one of them.

He made good progress. We were all really hopeful he would stay the course. Then on the morning of 5 May 2000 Bill asked to see me. I immediately noticed he was not dressed for work therapy and guessed he was intending to leave the programme.

Bill looked terrific – really fit and well. But from experience I knew he wasn't ready, not recovered enough to cope with the outside again. I tried to persuade him to stay even if only for another couple of weeks. Bill said: 'I've been to your lectures, Nick, and listened to all you have to say. You describe that amazing high that drinkers get from alcohol. Well, I get that. The only other thing in life that has ever given me that is the incredible buzz I get from being in the newsroom. I want that back . . .'

Bill, tragically, did not get that back. He had fallen into that trap of addiction from which I myself had managed to clamber out three decades before. Founding Chaucer was my own way back, built up from what was left of a derelict hospital with the help of generations of alcoholics like Bill.

As we strove to perfect our recovery programme, the government meanwhile chose to all but eradicate sensible aid for victims and instead extend licensing hours against unequivocal advice from health professionals.

The government's so-called 'Alcohol Strategy', published in 2004, devoted one paragraph to treatment and no budget for services such as Chaucer, despite the billions of pounds' worth of revenue that alcohol pours into government coffers.

'Care in the Community' legislation enacted a decade earlier delivered a deadly blow to those who were motivated to seek treatment but, like Bill, had run out of money to pay privately. There are very few residential places for alcohol treatment, unless you are rich, and even then the treatment on offer is highly suspect. In June 2005 I had twenty-three empty beds at Chaucer and over a hundred victims on a waiting list who had no hope of obtaining funding. Meanwhile, we do what we can.

Bill Frost will be remembered for many things I have no doubt. But for one of them, all alcoholics should be eternally grateful. His life has given us this biography written by his sister – a journalist, like Bill. While it is a tribute, it is also an object lesson in how a life of alcoholic excess so often ends in tragedy. Bill's addiction robbed the world of a brilliant mind and, when sober, a sensitive and thoughtful man.

Chaucer Clinic closed its doors due to lack of government funding in May 2005. The programme is now available for all on the internet (www.alcoholismtreatmentonline.com).

Acknowledgements

I would like to thank the following for their help in the writing of this book . . . firstly my husband, Christy, for his amazing love, support and doses of daily encouragement, daughters Maria and Katy and son Joseph for keeping me going. My publisher Judith Longman and agent Viv Schuster provided constant enthusiasm and backing. Fergal Keane offered kindness and assistance from the start.

Filmmaker David Monaghan prevented me from wavering as well as contributing his insightful thoughts on reading the manuscript. Without the help of Danny McGrory I could not have discovered the whole of Bill's story, while Patrick Bishop, Alan Copps and Richard Duce also donated their time and memories. Friends and colleagues at the *Daily Mail* were deeply sympathetic and understanding.

I am grateful to friends Richard and Beverley Hearn, and Rhodri and Barbara Lewis for their constant affection both for me and my brother, Marco Pierre White for his belief in the author and her project, painter Richard Gorman for his emails of reassurance from around the world, Cathrine Sayer for her letters from home, Franca and Jinnie for their empathy throughout. I thank Alex and Kevin Hanley for talking to me.

Credit is due to Mike Torpy, Anil Gogna and Jan Marszewski from HM C & E for giving in to my persistence, and to the staff of Miss U, Tooting, for production support.

Special thanks to my cousin Dr Sheilagh Frost, Robin LeFever from the Promis Recovery Centre, the management of Times Newspapers, and Nick Charles, founder of the Chaucer Clinic, for their assistance before and after Bill's death.

Recent Perennials from Seed